The Wee Green Book

The extraordinary story of Glasgow Green: Britain's oldest public park

NEIL BAXTER

with

DONNY O'ROURKE

First published 2007 by
Neil Baxter Associates, Glasgow
on behalf of Glasgow City Council

Text: Neil Baxter (mail@neilbaxterassoc.co.uk)
Design: Jon Jardine (mail@jonjardine.com)

ISBN: 978-0-9537149-2-6

A catalogue record for this book is available from the British Library.

*We are grateful to the following people and organisations for the use of the photographs in this book:
Alan Crumlish; Michael Dale; Pete Downing; Anthony Duda (anthony@duda.fsbusiness.co.uk);
Glasgow City Council, Land Services; Glasgow City Council (Museums);
Glasgow City Council, Mitchell Library, Archives and Special Collections;
Glasgow School of Art Archives; Glasgow University Library, Special Collections;
Jon Jardine; Marsh's Library, Dublin; Jeff Smith; Ian Watson.*

*Glasgow Green Renewal Funders: European Regional Development Fund,
Glasgow Cty Council, Heritage Lottery Fund, The Headley Trust,
Historic Scotland, The 1805 Club*

ACKNOWLEDGEMENTS

This little book was commissioned as part of the Glasgow Green Renewal Project. While the restoration of the landscape and monuments of the Green were the primary focus of that endeavour, the value of the Green's heritage and the need to provide informative interpretation was a priority from the outset.

The Councillors charged with the care of Glasgow's parks have been fully supportive of the need to communicate Glasgow Green's history to a much wider audience. Initially, Councillor Alistair Watson helped to give the Green's renewal high priority among the city's aspirations and to secure funding. His successor, Councillor Aileen Colleran, has provided astute steering throughout. The senior officers within Glasgow City Council Land Services – Robert Booth, Director, and Ian Telford, Head of Project Management – have given detailed guidance on each element of the interpretation and have helped to steer the project. The officer charged with delivery of the renewal project, Pete Downing, has been a consistently inspiring, constructive and knowledgeable client throughout the long process of researching the Green and implementing its interpretation – on the ground, in various publications, online and on DVD. To him an especial thanks.

In addition to those mentioned above, a number of others have made valuable contributions. Donny O'Rourke provided much of the material in the chapters on *Preaching, Politics and Performance* and *Love, Literature and Laundry*. Indeed their authorship is predominantly to his credit. Early research was undertaken by the late Bobby Paterson, whose sensitivity and humour is much missed and who might well have added the title of Glasgow historian to his long list of creative credits. Tim Edwards, Ann Parsonage and George Parsonage applied their knowledge to the draft, a process that resulted in significant improvements. Theresa White produced and amended numerous typescripts and demonstrated extraordinary tolerance over successive revisions and amendments. Jon Jardine has, as ever, managed to wrap these words up within a design that enhances them immensely.

All history casts up challenges and contradictions, not least recent history where, ironically, accurate dates seem to take a lower priority. There are no less than three published dates for Michael Jackson's appearance at Glasgow Green. I sincerely hope that the date published here is correct and indeed that the many other facts quoted in this book are accurate. Each of those mentioned above has made a major contribution to ensuring that this little book tells the story of the Green in a lively and engaging way. However, the checking of the facts has been entirely my own responsibility.

Neil Baxter, February 2007

The Glasgow Show 2005

Contents

McLennan Arch

Preface

In 1999, work started on one of the most ambitious renovation projects ever undertaken on a city park in the UK. The renewal of Glasgow Green has restored this extraordinary park as an attraction not only for Glaswegians but also for visitors from around the world.

Glasgow Green now benefits from imaginative new planting schemes, enhanced play and event provision, restored monuments and informative interpretation. All this will help ensure that the Green, which played a crucial part in Glasgow's past, will continue to play a central role in the city's future.

The restored Glasgow Green is a place to gather, for strolling, for taking the air and a focus of fun for locals and visitors, young and old alike. It is also a landscape rich in history, a site of conflicts and of peace rallies; of protest and celebration; a focus for industry and leisure; a place of sporting exertion and peaceful contemplation.

Many of those who have visited this ancient parkland are among the most notable names in human history. Events that occurred here have helped to shape the modern world. Some would claim that this is the most historically resonant landscape in Scotland, if not in the whole of the UK!

This little book is designed, not as a definitive history of the Green, rather to give a flavour of the extraordinarily rich history of Britain's oldest park.

Councillor Aileen Colleran,
Executive Member for Parks, Glasgow City Council

The Glasgow Show 2005

Foreword

THE WEE GREEN BOOK, the first historical account of Glasgow Green in over two decades, follows the worthy endeavour of Hugh MacDonald's *Rambles Round Glasgow in the 1850s*. MacDonald's collection of essays includes a brilliant account of the history of the Green and its mid-nineteenth century role in the life of the city, the first detailed literary exploration of the history of a landscape that has witnessed events of world significance.

The much more recent publications by the Friends of the People's Palace (*Glasgow Green and Roundabout, a Tourist Guide,* 1982) and Elspeth King (*The People's Palace and Glasgow Green,* 1985) give superb insights into the late twentieth century role of Glasgow's oldest park. However, both of these accounts were written at a time of uncertainty, when the Winter Gardens was under threat and the Doulton Fountain but a shattered remnant of its former glory. Now both the Winter Gardens and the fountain are gloriously restored, as is the Green itself – a worthy moment to celebrate its extraordinary history.

Neil Baxter

The Glasgow Humane Society Pontoon

Introduction

FOR FIVE AND A HALF CENTURIES, Glasgow Green has served the people of Glasgow. Beyond its utilitarian uses, the grazing of cattle and the washing and bleaching of linen, the Green's history reflects every aspect of Glasgow's social, economic, political and cultural life. Indeed, over the centuries, this 136 acres of parkland, by the banks of the Clyde, has played host to politicians, sportsmen, entertainers, innovators and events of world significance.

It is fitting, in a city which achieved world prominence through industry, that Glasgow Green might legitimately lay claim to be the birthplace of the industrial revolution. It was here, on a Sunday afternoon stroll in 1765, that James Watt had the inspiration for the steam engine that would, quite literally, power Britain to industrial ascendancy in the century that followed. Here, too, the workers of Glasgow would gather to demand improvements in their pay and living conditions. Thus the Green also witnessed the dawning of workers' rights and the Labour movement.

A third, crucial, strand in the industrial mix, undoubtedly influenced by the often vociferous dissent of Glasgow's workforce, was the birth of enlightened capitalism. In this, too, Glasgow Green played its part. One of the earliest champions of this approach, the banker, industrialist and philanthropist David Dale, set up home beside the Green in the early 1780s.

Yet while it may be credited as the birthplace of the industrial revolution, the Green has also had its share of notable visitors. The Green played its part in the lives of two of Scotland's most famous royal figures. In 1568, Regent Moray assembled his army here before defeating Mary, Queen of Scots, at the Battle of Langside. The connection with Prince Charles Edward Stuart is more direct. In early 1746, smarting from defeat at Derby, Bonnie Prince Charlie marched his troops up and down the Green threatening to destroy the city. More peaceful visitors of world renown have included Benjamin Franklin, William Wordsworth and, in more recent years, Mother Teresa of Calcutta. Highlighting the Green's more contemporary and settled role as a place for leisure and recreation, performers who have drawn huge crowds in recent years include Michael Jackson and Marilyn Manson.

The Green's role as a focus for public events has ranged from its sinister use as the venue for public hangings to the more upbeat annual Glasgow Fair. It has witnessed countless political and religious gatherings. Adding to this rich mix the Green is now a popular venue for major open-air concerts, Maydaze and Pride events, the World Pipe Band Championships and Glasgow's annual fireworks celebration.

Another centuries-old tradition is the use of the Green for sport. In 1850 Hugh MacDonald commented on the 'healthful and exciting games' including cricket, rounders, football, shinty and golf which regularly featured on the Green. Indeed Glasgow's oldest park played an important role in the founding of Rangers Football Club. In addition to its continuing role as a focus of football, the Green hosts the finish of the annual Great Scottish Run and continues to support the long tradition of rowing on the Clyde.

As the great Glasgow poet and songsmith, Adam McNaughtan, has observed, other landscapes, particularly battle scenes, earn renown for a single event in their history. He wryly comments on

The Knights of the Damned, The Glasgow Show 2005

tourists visiting Bannockburn and Culloden Moor to recall their famous battles, yet,

> *"These places just have one event,*
> *That makes them worth being seen,*
> *A thousand years of history*
> *Have marked the Glasgow Green!"* [1]

1 Adam McNaughtan, quoted in Elspeth King, *The People's Palace and Glasgow Green*, 1985 p20

Illustration of Glasgow Green from a round box lid, c. 1830s

ONE

A Precious Green Place

THE STORY OF GLASGOW GREEN begins on 20 April 1450 with the granting of land by James II (1430-1460) to William Turnbull, Bishop of Glasgow. While the Green is not mentioned by name most subsequent accounts assume that it was included in King James' gift:

> *"We have given to the said Bishop and his successors forever, the City of Glasgow, Barony of Glasgow, and lands commonly called the Bishop's Forest with their pertinents in woods, planes, meadows, marsh's, pasturages…"* [2]

At that time, the Green bore little resemblance to the modern day parkland that bears the name. Indeed for several centuries afterwards the areas identified as High Green, Low (or Laigh) Green, and Gallowgate (or Calton) Green grew and contracted as land was built upon, sold off and re-acquired by the City Fathers.

2 Hugh MacDonald, *Rambles Round Glasgow in the 1850s:* The Public Green.

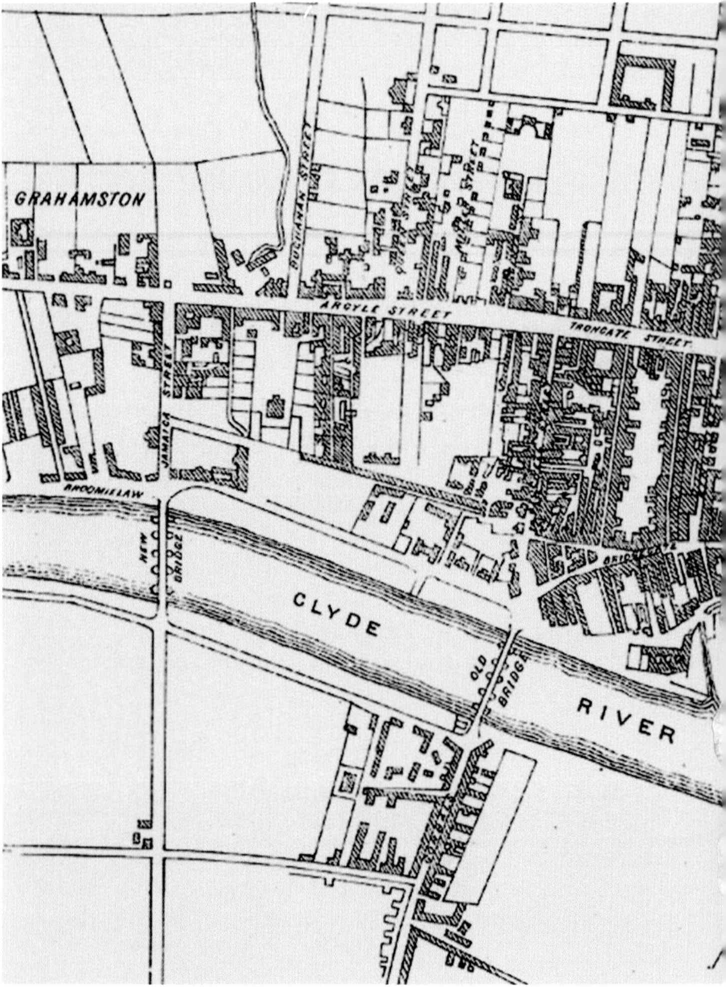

Plan of the City of Glasgow, 1783

HIGH STREET
GALLOWGATE STREET
SALT MARKET STREET
CALTON
WASHING HOUSE
LOW GREEN
GALLOWGATE GREEN
HIGH GREEN
CLYDE RIVER

One relatively early indication of the development of the Green as a leisure ground was the laying out of tree-lined serpentine walks by Lord Provost George Murdoch in 1756. Unfortunately, as Hugh MacDonald was later to record, these were subject to 'abuses' and removed. The Green only achieved its present day scale and something like its current form after the purchase of King's Park in 1773 from John King, Deacon of the Guild of Fleshers, the founding of McPhun's Park by Robert McPhun, owner of Greenhead Sawmills, and the subsequent purchase of Fleshers' Haugh from Patrick Bell of Cowcaddens in 1792.

Throughout the eighteenth and nineteenth centuries, the Green combined its role as a pleasure ground with much more utilitarian usage as a washing ground and a pasture for grazing sheep and cattle. During the twentieth century the stretch of the Green beside the Clyde, eastward of Nelson's Monument, provided allotments where people from both the Gorbals and Calton areas grew vegetables; a particular boon during the war years.

In his *History of Glasgow* (1736), John M'Ure wrote of the Green:

> *"Adorned with pleasant galleries of elm-trees, and situated upon the south-east corner of the city, and is inclosed with a stately stone-wall, 2,500 ells* [3] *in length, and fenced on the south with the river of Clyde, it hath all the summer time betwixt two and three hundred women bleaching of linen cloth, and washing linen cloths of all sorts in the river Clyde... there is a lodge built of free-stone in the midst of it, for a shelter to the herd who waits upon the horse and cows that are grassed therein."* [4]

3 An ell was equivalent to six hand breadths, about 45 inches (115 centimetres)

4 *The History of Glasgow* (John M'Ure), Glasgow 1736, Reprinted 1830 p121.

Glasgow Green *c.1800, watercolour by Hugh William Williams*

A fixed rate was charged for each animal kept on the Green, that for cattle being twenty shillings a head. A herd who supervised this public amenity was accommodated in the shed beside the future site of Nelson's Monument. This bore the rather misleading title 'The Herd's House' but was in reality, as M'Ure observed, little more than a shelter from the rain.

The system changed in 1746 when the last herd, John Picken, was dismissed. The horn that he used in the execution of his duties still survives in the collection of the People's Palace. However, the grazing of cattle continued until 1870 and sheep much longer. The City's accounts record that by the 1890s annual income from the grazing of sheep totalled 42 pounds and 10 shillings.

Yet the Green was home to much more commercial activity than simply the grazing of cattle. Fleshers' Haugh in particular was the

Glasgow Bridges and the Merchants' Tower *by J Brooks, c. 1806*

focus for a whole range of industries including tar pits, glue works and tripe houses. The gore and stench were horrendous:

> *"The dung of the Slaughter House, and the intestines of slaughtered animals, were collected in heaps, and allowed to remain for months together, till putrefaction took place, to the great annoyance of the neighbourhood".* [5]

Although the public was used to the dirt and stench of industry, Glasgow Green was particularly unsavoury and, in 1810, a clean-up was ordered. Over the next two decades, under the direction of Dr. James Cleland, Glasgow's Superintendent of Public Works, major improvements were carried out. By 1828, the Green was transformed.

5 *Old Glasgow and Its Environs* by Senex (Robert Reid), 1864 p60.

Cleland's improvements reinforced the Green's status as Glasgow's people's park. The folk of Bridgeton, Calton and Gorbals in particular were fiercely protective of the Green's rolling landscape. In the early years of the nineteenth century the local textile merchant, Alexander Allan, stirred up huge indignation by his re-routing of pedestrian traffic through a short tunnel or 'pen' at the eastern end of the Green to give himself exclusive access to the Clyde from his mansion at Newhall. So incensed were the weavers in Bridgeton and Calton that they refused to work for him and he was forced into bankruptcy. The Clyde, like the public, disapproved of Mr Allan's presumption, and only a year after it was built the river, in spate, washed Allan's pen away.

Dr. James Cleland 1770-1840

Glasgow, *Engraving by S. Davenport, 1834*

Local landowners were far from the only threats to the Green. In 1821 a survey, ironically undertaken by James Cleland, the man who had done so much to improve the Green, revealed that beneath its trees, walks and verdant pastures lay huge seams of coal. Some members of the Council greeted the news that as much as one and half million tons of black gold lay beneath the Green with the predictably pragmatic response that this was an asset of greater value than any park. Happily, public pressure saved Glasgow Green from being transformed into a giant open cast coal mine in the 1820s. However, it was a threat that would recur regularly throughout the nineteenth century.

Another radical proposal, which would have destroyed the Green, was that this should be the site of Glasgow's main port. The idea was first mooted by engineer and inventor Henry Bell, of *Bell's Comet* fame. Fortunately, the proposal was soon vigorously rebutted

View from Arns Well, *Drawn by John Fleming, engraved by Joseph Swan, 1830s*

McLennan Arch, Monteith Row, c. 1900

by a vociferous local environmental lobby. The civil engineer, Jesse Hartley, presented a further report in April 1834, which advocated that the Green would provide 'the most proper place' for a major expansion of the city's dock facilities. This notion too was rapidly shelved after the first stirrings of public indignation.

In 1857, Glasgow Green finally achieved official designation as a public park. However, only a year later, the advocates of an alternative future for the Green as a landscape blighted by coal mining stepped up the pressure. The owner of the Milton Iron Works, John MacDowell, proposed mining the Green as a solution to the Council's massive £100,000 debt. The fact that this debt had been largely generated by the purchase of parkland for the West End and Southside was not lost on East End folk. Worse still, MacDowell's proposal was to back-fill any subsidence with 'waste deposits', the idea being to effectively transform Glasgow Green into a gigantic rubbish tip.

The local Councillor, Bailie James Moir, led vociferous public protest against MacDowell's plan. A protest song, *Airn John,* made it explicitly clear that (iron) John MacDowell would "never get the Glasgow Green to pay the West End Park." The people of the East End were determined to protect their own Dear Green Place:

"If ye maun sink a pit, John.
Sink it in George's Square,
Or sink it in the Crescents John,
Amang the rich folk there." [6]

Glasgow Green c. 1950

6 Elspeth King: *The People's Palace and Glasgow Green,* 1985 p31.

Happily, Moir and his fellow protestors succeeded. However, their achievement was all too soon forgotten and further public protest to prevent mining was required in 1869 and then again in 1888, when the idea of extracting Glasgow Green's coal seems finally to have been put to rest.

Another recurring threat to the uninterrupted landscape of the Green was the encroachment of major transport routes. In 1847, the Glasgow, Monkland and Airdrie Railway Company proposed to run a railway viaduct straight through the Green. On this occasion the proposal was thwarted in Parliament where Mr Austin QC passionately advocated the rights of the main beneficiaries of Glasgow Green – "the working classes."

In 1900, a major roadway connection was cut through Glasgow Green when King's Drive, linking Bridgeton to Hutchesontown, effectively separated Fleshers' Haugh from the rest of the Green. This disconnection of the Haugh might account for the proposals, many decades later, to develop this particular area for distinctly different uses from the rest of the Green.

In 1988, a Council plan proposed an ambitious leisure development at the Haugh. As with so many other issues in the Green's long history, the proposal was met with vehement public protest and, eventually, rejected. The subsequent transformation of the Haugh's blaes pitches to their present day use as Glasgow Green Football Centre, complete with eighteen pitches (some grass, others synthetic), was presumably felt to be a much more appropriate style of development and progressed without demur.

The latter part of the twentieth century produced several other threats to the integrity of the Green. The architect Sam Bunton proposed the building of a series of multi-storey blocks on what he considered prime development land. Happily this radical notion was rejected as an absurd flight of architectural fancy. More threatening

Topiary Avenue

was the 1970s proposal to create the eastern flank of the proposed Inner Ring Road which would have cut a north-south scar across the Green just in front of Nelson's Monument. The Secretary of State for Scotland deferred that plan in 1981, effectively ending a long period of uncertainty.

The next chapter in Glasgow Green's rich history is a great deal happier. In the mid 1990s the City Council announced ambitious plans to regenerate the Green. Supported by funding from a number of sources, the Council embarked upon a meticulous process of restoring the landscape and monuments that embody Glasgow Green's proud history. Debris from World War II air-raid shelters was removed, contours re-arranged and the ground itself reinforced. Now new fencing encloses renewed carriageways and paths, while attractive new lighting and seating ensures public comfort.

The day-to-day use of the Green as a public park has been reinforced by the transplanting of 115 existing trees and planting

Relaxing on the Green

of nearly 550 new, semi-mature specimens. One crucial role of the Green, which has been enhanced by the subtle re-shaping of the landscape, is its role as a venue for major events. Fifty percent of Glasgow Green's total area is now available for festivals, performances and celebrations.

The renewal of Glasgow Green recognises the rich history of this extraordinary place. For generations, the Green has been fiercely protected by local people who have seen off threats from mining, development, railways and roads. Now, gloriously restored, the Green remains Glasgow's unique people's park.

Ben Parsonage (1903-1979) March 1958

TWO

History and Heroes

THROUGHOUT ITS LONG HISTORY, Glasgow Green has been visited by numerous figures whose world fame, or notoriety, endures. Many others who played a prominent role in the story of the Green in centuries past are long forgotten. However, few landscapes have played host to such a rich variety of royal visitors, literati, scientists, preachers, politicians, protestors, sporting heroes and pop stars. Many of these visitors make their appearance in the chapters that follow. However, there are some figures of international renown and other local heroes whose contribution to the history of the Green or of Glasgow is distinctive and particular. Their stories do not sit easily under any general heading. Indeed each of them has made a special contribution to Glasgow Green's claim to be among the world's most significant historic sites.

Among the earliest recorded visitors to the Green was Mary, Queen of Scots' half brother, Regent Moray. Moray had been Queen Mary's advisor. However, he opposed her marriage to Lord Darnley and was exiled to England. After Mary's forced abdication in 1567, he was appointed Regent of Scotland. In early May 1568,

Charles Edward Stuart 1720-1788

Mary escaped from imprisonment at Loch Leven and gathered an army of Catholic nobles in an attempt to regain the throne. Moray and the Protestant lords assembled their forces on Glasgow Green. On 13 May 1568, they set off from the Green to engage with Mary's army at the Battle of Langside where Mary was finally defeated and fled south to England. Ironically, she outlived her half brother. He was assassinated by one of her supporters in Linlithgow in 1570 while Scotland's erstwhile Queen lived on for nearly twenty years, until her execution in 1587.

A more direct royal association, and a thoroughly unwelcome one at the time, arose when Prince Charles Edward Stuart arrived in Glasgow in the winter of 1745. He had been defeated at the Battle of Derby and his troops were in a sorry state. Bonnie Prince Charlie himself took up residence at Shawfield Mansion on Glassford Street while his bedraggled army settled wherever they could in the precincts of the Green, some taking shelter in the part-built walls of the nearby St. Andrew's-in-the-Square. The Prince effectively held the city to ransom, demanding 12,000 shirts and 6,000 coats, pairs of shoes, stockings, waistcoats and bonnets as well as supplies to sustain his army for their onward march.

On 2nd January 1746, standing at a spot at the western edge of Fleshers' Haugh, the Prince reviewed his newly re-attired troops, who marched out, according to one of the Prince's English followers,

> *"With drums beating, colours flying, bagpipes playing and all the marks of a triumphant army, to the appointed ground, attended by multitudes of people who had come from all parts to see us, and especially the ladies, who, though formerly much against us, were now changed by the sight of the Prince into the most enthusiastic loyalty".* [7]

The Prince himself was particularly admired. During his stay, Bonnie Prince Charlie was introduced to a local merchant's daughter, Clementina Walkinshaw, who became his mistress. She later travelled to Rome to live with him and bore him a daughter. Others felt pity for the Prince. A local witness commented on the Prince's nobility but reckoned that the Prince had the air of a man who knew his cause was lost and

> *"Seemed to have a melancholy foreboding of that disaster which soon after ruined the hopes of his family forever".* [8]

7 Hugh MacDonald, *Rambles Round Glasgow in the 1850s: The Public Green*
8 Hugh MacDonald, *Op Cit*

Dissuaded from sacking and burning the city by the compliance of the City Fathers to his demands, Charles and his army left for Stirling on 3 January. Predictably, his defeat at Culloden on 16 April 1746 was an occasion for much celebration in Glasgow. Some three years later the Council's appeal to Parliament recovered a large part of the financial loss it had suffered at the hands of the Jacobites.

James Watt 1736-1819

Only twenty years on from the Jacobite siege, in more peaceful times, the Green played a crucial role in an event that would change the course of world history. On a Sunday afternoon stroll, early in 1765, James Watt, perhaps reflecting on the tradition of washing at the Green, was inspired with the idea that led to the invention of his highly effective steam engine. This discovery would play a central role in Britain's development as the world's most powerful industrial nation for well over a century to come.

Born in Greenock in 1736, Watt had already achieved some success as a scientific instrument maker and the retailer of 'mathematical and musical instruments' as well as toys and novelties. Glasgow University had given him premises to help him set up and continued to be a major client. The University owned a model of Thomas Newcomen's famous, but also famously inefficient, steam engine that was in need of repair. Watt prevailed upon his friend John Anderson, the Professor of Natural Philosophy, to give him the model, which he soon repaired.

Watt knew that the design of Newcomen's engine was flawed. It consumed huge quantities of coal and its boilers tended to overheat and burn out. Watt realised that the introduction of a separate condensing chamber would save fuel by maintaining the temperature of the primary cylinder. It was to take a further decade and a move to Birmingham for Watt's invention to start achieving its potential. However, by the end of his life he was considered among the greatest scientists of his age and universally admired.

In 1818, a year before Watt's death, he attended a gathering along with a number of Scotland's great and good, including Sir Walter Scott. Scott described James Watt as,

> *"This magician whose cloudy machinery has produced a change in the world… the most profound man of science – the most successful combiner of powers and calculator of numbers as applied to practical purposes…"* [9]

Watt's engine was among the inventions which, quite literally, powered Britain's industrial revolution. Its significance was such that there are two memorials to James Watt on Glasgow Green. The first, a life-sized stone statue by the sculptor Charles Grassby, was presented to the city in 1936. The statue was originally sited over the gateway of W & J Martin's Leatherworks at Baltic Street, Bridgeton. When their premises were being rebuilt, the company gifted the statue to the city. It shows Watt holding a pair of dividers while resting his right arm on a large steam cylinder.

Originally erected in McPhun's Park at the eastern extremity of the Green, the Watt statue had been attacked by vandals so, by the time of its removal to its new site beside the People's Palace, it required significant repair, including a new head. Now re-capitated,

9 Thomas Somerville, George Square, Glasgow, 1891 p99.

James Watt stands close to the site of his original inspiration. However, the supposedly exact spot is marked by the second memorial to Watt, a boulder that was set in place in 1965, marking the bicentenary of Watt's inspiration on Glasgow Green.

A far more spectacular demonstration of the wonders of science was the balloon ascent of a figure who was among the most famous of his age, the daredevil aeronaut, Vincenzo Lunardi. On 23rd November 1785, Lunardi's extraordinary hot air balloon, an impressive construction of 520 yards of green, yellow and pink oiled silk, took off from the churchyard at St. Andrew's-in-the-Square.

The event prompted one of the greatest gatherings of Glasgow's citizens ever seen. Virtually the whole of the city's population witnessed the spectacle. Servants abandoned their duties and workers ceased their toil to view this amazing feat of bravado.

At 1:45 on that fine November afternoon, Lunardi's flight took off to gasps of amazement from the ground. After a rapid ascent, the balloon drifted off southward. Over the next two hours, its rapid progress was witnessed by the amazed townsfolk of first Hamilton and then Lanark before Lunardi touched down, happily unscathed, in Hawick.

M. Lunardi's triumph has, like his gaudy craft, drifted into obscurity, little more than an historical footnote. However, the great French aeronaut is commemorated in the poetry of Robert Burns. In *To A Louse* (1786), Burns feigns affront at the impudence of the flea which, rather than settling upon some suitably downtrodden representative of the human species, chooses to settle upon the, presumably balloon-like, bonnet of a high-born young lady,

> *"But Miss's fine Lunardi fye!*
> *How daur ye do't?"* [10]

10 Sydney Goodsir Smith (Editor), *Burns's Poems and Songs* (London, 1966)

One likely witness to Lunardi's triumph would have been the industrialist and entrepreneur David Dale who, five years earlier, had taken up residence at the foot of Charlotte Street. The area had previously been a fruit and vegetable market before being laid out as a gated street of large mansion houses. Dale's mansion, facing the Green, was the most opulent in the street. He had commissioned the leading architect of the age, Robert Adam, to build his home, in the popular Palladian, Italianate style of the day, for a huge budget of £6,000.

David Dale 1739-1806, medallion by Tassie

Dale, son of an Ayrshire shopkeeper, had begun his working life as a herd-boy then took to weaving before becoming an importer of Dutch and French linen. In 1783, he invited the Lancastrian inventor Richard Arkwright to visit him in Glasgow. He took Arkwright to a site near the Falls of Clyde at Lanark which, because of its damp river valley setting and the availability of water power, seemed to Dale to be the ideal place to establish a cotton mill.

The two men formed a short-lived partnership, but New Lanark was destined to be a huge success. By the time Dale sold the mill to his son-in-law, the Welshman Robert Owen, New Lanark was employing 1,300 adults and over 400 pauper children. Dale had also inaugurated the care and education systems that established his reputation as a pioneer of social welfare.

David Dale was a rotund and well-liked figure. With his cocked hat and cane, he was a familiar sight around the Saltmarket and, it seems, inspired the character of Bailie Nicol Jarvie in Sir Walter

David Dale's mansion

Scott's *Rob Roy*. He was also a non-conformist preacher. Those who heard him complimented his plain speaking, his earnestness and his reliance on his scriptural sources. However, it seems that, although fervent in his belief, he was never a truly charismatic orator.

Another aspect of David Dale's extraordinarily full life was his role as an agent for the Royal Bank of Scotland. It was when acting in this capacity, on 18 November 1795, that Dale managed to transform what might have been a social disaster into something of a triumph. He had been organising a grand dinner at his home for the directors of the Royal Bank, some Glasgow businessmen and other friends and colleagues. Dale's servants were preparing a great feast of spit-roasted joints of meat, boiled stuffed turkeys and a wealth of trimmings.

All day the rain fell and the Clyde threatened to breach its banks. This was not an unusual event – Glasgow Green was a notorious floodplain. A previous great flood in March 1782 had inundated both Gorbals and the whole of the East End of the city. However, in 1795 a quite unprecedented new calamity struck. The Monkland Canal, completed just the year before, also burst its banks. The Molendinar Burn brought a torrent of water down through the city's eastern flank. Many insubstantial houses in Gallowgate, Saltmarket and Bridgegate were flooded and destroyed. The waters that had been oozing into David Dale's house inundated the kitchen in a great rush, putting out the fires.

Ever the pragmatist, Dale sought the use of two of his neighbours' kitchens. However, by this time his wine cellar was under four feet of water and, no longer a young man, he felt unable to venture below himself to fetch the port, sherry and madeira for dinner. The solution was to send his daughter, then aged sixteen, down, mounted on the back of a servant. Between them, they managed to identify and retrieve the required bottles. The dinner was saved,

> *"And the whole party passed the evening in mirth and jocularity at the odd circumstances which had attended the merry evening".* [11]

While intermittent inundation was undoubtedly inconvenient, it was not the reason for David Dale's eventual departure from Charlotte Street. By the end of the eighteenth century, the growth in industry in the area – particularly chemical works, tanneries and the glue works at Fleshers' Haugh – created a permanent stench that forced the wealthy to move out. In 1799, the same year as the marriage of his plucky daughter, Caroline, to Robert Owen, and

11 Senex (Robert Reid), *Old Glasgow and Its Environs*, 1864 p121

Maggie McIver (1879-1958) and Barrowland

The Barras

his sale of New Lanark to his son-in-law, David Dale moved to Cambuslang, where he stayed until his death in 1806.

His house was later to become Glasgow's Eye Infirmary. It was subsequently occupied by the Salvation Army before its demolition, in 1954, to make way for the extension of Our Lady and St. Francis Secondary School.

Around a century after David Dale's departure from Glasgow Green, another entrepreneur, whose impact locally would be no less enduring, settled in the area. Maggie Russell, who was born in Galston in Ayrshire, the daughter of a policeman, married James McIver in 1897. Maggie McIver would, in time, earn renown as the founder of the famous Barras Market.

In the early days, Maggie built a rental business with street barrows for which she charged threepence per day or eightpence for a week. As business progressed, she bought the ground upon which the market stood. By roofing over the area, she was able to establish the Barras on a more permanent basis and, on a neighbouring site, built the famous Barrowland Ballroom.

The Barrowland opened to great fanfare on Christmas Eve 1934 and for many years was one of Glasgow's most popular dance halls with its resident band, Billy McGregor and the Gaybirds. Maggie died in 1958, ironically in the same year as the original Barrowland Ballroom was destroyed by fire. However, two years later its replacement opened, its façade on Gallowgate brilliantly lit in a competition-winning neon design.

Maggie McIver might justifiably be described as the most influential Green-side entrepreneur of the last century. However, the most famous twentieth century resident of Glasgow Green was Ben Parsonage, for over fifty years the Officer of Glasgow Humane Society. The Society had its origins in a legacy of £200 from James Coulter in 1787 who stipulated that this very significant sum should be used to 'set up a society for the rescue of drowning persons'.

George Parsonage, 2005

In August 1787, a meeting was held in the Tontine Hotel at Trongate to inaugurate the Society and, by 1790, Glasgow Humane Society was fully established. Five years later in 1795, the Society built its first boathouse on the Clyde and a house on Glasgow Green. In the same year, the Society's first Officer, John Wiseman, was appointed, somehow balancing his life-saving role with working as a shoemaker in the Saltmarket. Within the first thirty years of the Humane Society's existence over 600 lives were saved.

George Geddes was appointed the Society's Officer in 1859. His son, also named George, succeeded him in the post in 1889. The younger George Geddes remained in the post for a remarkable forty years. His son, also George, became the Assistant Officer of the Society; sadly, the daily danger faced by the officers of the Humane Society was demonstrated by his death by drowning in 1928. Over the next fifty years, George Geddes' successor, Ben Parsonage, supported by his wife Sarah, rescued over 1,500 people in danger of drowning in the Clyde. When Ben Parsonage died in 1979, he was succeeded by his son George, who has himself rescued over 1,500 people from the Clyde.

THREE

Preaching, Politics and Performance

THESE DAYS THE CITY usually gets by with only a third of its motto: "Lord, Let Glasgow Flourish by the Preaching of Thy Word and the Praising of Thy Name". Nevertheless, from the time of St. Mungo until today, preaching, both religious and secular, has been very important to Glasgow and much of that oratory was to be heard on Glasgow Green – the second city's Hyde Park Corner.

Even before the Green was formally gifted to the city, it was drawing hucksters and hecklers, churchmen and chancers, dissidents and demagogues. The tradition of preaching on the Green is an ancient one, though sadly the chronicler of Glasgow's saints, Jocelin of Furness, does not record whether Columba or Mungo preached by the Clyde. However, it is more than likely that the Green witnessed its share of conversions among the local pagan population. Later the Franciscans, and especially the Dominicans, whose specific historic ministry is preaching, may well have gathered crowds of the God-fearing, and perhaps even the occasional scoffer, to listen on the banks of the Clyde.

In the bitter religious disputes during the reigns of Charles II and James II (of Great Britain, 1633-1701) the fervent, Presbyterian Covenanters often railed on the Green against the idea of Bishops, whether Roman Catholic or Anglican. Many martyrs were executed in Glasgow. The present day Martyrs Church at Townhead is close to the original site for executions in Glasgow. The Martyrs stone there marks the executions, in 1684, of James Nisbet, James Lawson and Alexander Wood.

During the centuries-long quarrel between England and Scotland – not even ended by the accession to the British throne of the Scottish King in 1603 – the Green provided a venue for much passion and patriotism.

The Green itself was the focus of much religious fervour. However, from the mid-eighteenth century onwards, worship went indoors and the area saw the development of several fine churches. Scotland's first purpose-built Episcopalian church opened in 1750. Its name, St. Andrew-by-the-Green, proclaims its proximity. The interior of this little classical building boasted unprecedented levels of luxury, including cushioning on the pews. When an organ was installed in 1775, it became known by the disdainful nickname, the "Whistlin' Kirk". Its builder, Andrew Hunter, was excommunicated by the Shuttle Street Presbyterian Church for his involvement in this theologically dubious enterprise.

The nearby St. Andrew's-in-the-Square, with its magnificent tower and lofty, columned portico, was modelled on St. Martin-in-the-Fields in London's Trafalgar Square. The work of Allan Dreghorn and the master mason Mungo Nasmith, this Presbyterian church features subtle and restrained wood and plasterwork, alongside more lavish later carving and stained glass. Standing just a few yards away from the first St. Andrew's, this much grander enterprise took seventeen years, from 1739 to 1756, to finish.

The Tent Hall, Steel Street, c. 1920

From 1790, the city's first Baptists, referred to as 'Scotch Baptists' to distinguish them from their English brethren, were immersed in the Clyde at Fleshers' Haugh. From the 1790s onwards, Roman Catholics from the Highlands and Ireland were also drawn to the East End. The first post-Reformation Catholic Church was situated in Marshall's Lane in the Calton near the Green, the only place of worship for Catholics until the building, by subscription in 1816, of what would, in time, become St. Andrew's Cathedral. This, the third important church in the area to bear the name of Scotland's patron saint, stands on Clyde Street not far away from its namesakes.

Glasgow's largest gospel hall also has connections with the Green. Originally operating from a tent on the Green itself, the Glasgow United Evangelical Association consolidated the success of the massive Evangelical revival of 1874-5, by constructing what became known as the 'Tent Hall' on Steel Street. Its focus was the working poor of the city, a congregation that some longer-established churches had neglected. In later years, the building was occupied by the YMCA before being converted to flats in 2003.

Until the nineteenth century, 'compurgators' patrolled the Green each Sunday during 'Kirk hours' to ensure that everyone was either at church or at home. Outwith 'Kirk hours' the Green hosted several celebrity speakers. In *From Glasgow's Treasure Chest*, James Cowan conjectures that John Wesley would have repaired to the Saracen's Head Inn for a taste of its famous well water, and maybe something stronger, after preaching on the Green in the course of one of the great Methodist tours. This most spellbinding of preachers visited Scotland twenty-two times between 1751 and 1790.

It was the gospel of Catholic emancipation and Irish home rule that Daniel O'Connell preached to an appreciative crowd of the Glasgow Irish and others sympathetic to reform. Not everyone converging on the Green agreed with O'Connell's ideas: the 'happy bigot', Harry Long, protested vociferously against the restoration of the Scottish Roman Catholic Church hierarchy. In 1878, a rally on the Green protested against the installation of the Most Rev. Charles Eyre as Glasgow's Archbishop, which was cited as an act of 'papal aggression'. Long, a director of the Glasgow Working Men's Evangelistic Association, was still rousing his followers in the 1880s with the slogan, "no concession to potpourri". While some, understandably, considered his views offensive, others commended him as a defender of the faith. His portrait bust, in white marble, is on show in the People's Palace.

Daniel O'Connell's near namesake, the firebrand Chartist leader, Daniel O'Connor, attracted a huge crowd to the Green in 1835, joined on an ecumenical platform by the rector of Paisley Abbey, the Reverend Patrick Brooster, and the Lord Provost of Glasgow's son, George Miller. "Rarely has Great Britain been so close to revolution as in those 1830s", commented Charles Oakley in his important Glasgow history, *The Second City*.

The Green had played its part, over forty years before, in Glasgow's first recorded strike. On 30 June 1787, seven thousand weavers, angered by a cut in their wages, gathered on the Green. They resolved to strike. In early September six weavers were killed and many seriously injured when the strike was broken in a violent confrontation.

The Calton Weavers' strike undoubtedly contributed to the anti-combination laws in the early nineteenth century which made assembling to listen to speeches highly dangerous. This had also been the case in the 1790s, when the example of France and the writings of Tom Paine had would-be insurgents hanging on every word of those who risked transportation or execution to bring their egalitarian message to the Green. There are however ambiguities here, as typified by the presence on the Green of the Nelson Monument, the first memorial in Britain to the Vice Admiral to be funded by popular subscription. Glasgow's ambivalent attitude to Bonaparte is also borne out by the well-attended patriotic review on the Green in 1804.

The mob could be fickle. In 1820, two miles of palings round the Green were pulled up and a huge bonfire lit in outrage at the treatment of Queen Caroline, the estranged wife of George IV. A bridge collapsed under the weight of the crowds fleeing the militia. Perhaps the most alarming riot occurred in 1848, when the hordes streaming from the Green erected barricades in the Gallowgate and 10,000 special constables had to be hastily sworn in.

The Chief of Police was forced to resign and the town guard fired on the protesters, killing several. This 'Bread Riot', caused, like so many contemporary protests, by want of food, was the most disturbing in the eyes of the government at Westminster until the

May Day meeting, 1913

events of 'Black Friday' in 1919 when tanks were sent in to George Square. The Clyde Workers Committee had called many meetings previously on the Green in pursuit of the forty-hour week and other demands. Its leaders, Emmanuel Shinwell, William Gallagher and David (Davie) Kirkwood spent many months in jail.

The energies and aspirations of Glasgow's early socialists found parliamentary expression in 1922, when the city sent ten Labour MPs to London, including the mesmeric orator James Maxton, a star turn on the Green. This sincerely socialist maverick proved less effective in the committee rooms than his colleague John Wheatley, a future Minister of Health and visionary provider of much municipal housing for the workers.

Glasgow's most mythologised and celebrated left wing firebrand, John MacLean, died just a year after the 'Clydesiders' took the train south, his health broken by his continuous struggle for the socialist cause and the brutality of prison. A champion of education for the workers, he was appointed by Comrade Lenin to the role of Bolshevik Consul to Scotland in 1917. MacLean's practical legacy may be small, but his legend is immense.

John MacLean 1879-1923

It was on Glasgow Green that MacLean had advocated a Scottish republic. As the politics preached there moved ever leftwards, a 1916 by-law was used to prohibit singing, preaching, lectures and demonstrating. After a long campaign, the Communist writer and editor of the newspaper, *The World*, Guy Aldred, had these ancient rights partially restored in March 1932.

Much of Glasgow's flourishing throughout the eighteenth century was attributable to the tobacco trade, a business impossible without some complicity in slavery. Attempts to bring about emancipation included many rallies on Glasgow Green. Following that struggle, the woman's suffrage movement was to last almost a century from its origins in the volatile 1830s. Once again, jail was no deterrent. Among the many Glasgow women who went to prison for their beliefs in the early twentieth century were the well-known actress, Maggie Moffat, and Dr. Elizabeth Chalmers Smith, one of the earliest female graduates in medicine at Glasgow University, wife of the progressive Minister of Calton Parish Church, an arsonist for the cause and later a pioneer of women's medicine in the city.

Guy Aldred leading a march to the Green, 1936

The wider Labour movement in the run-up to and beyond the First World War was sympathetic to the campaign for votes for woman. Tom Johnston's *Forward* newspaper was an eloquent source of support. All of those associated with what was to become "Red Clydeside" outlined their contrasting and competing versions of socialism on the Green.

The Green continued to serve as a political gathering place throughout the twentieth century. In 1920, a rally on the Green supported calls for a national general strike. In the decade that followed, despite the by-law prohibiting gatherings on the Green, a number of demonstrations demanded new jobs and support for the unemployed. However, perhaps the most impressive twentieth century gathering on the Green was to come several decades later.

On 18 August 1971, an estimated 80,000 marchers from throughout the UK gathered at George Square and set off to a great rally at Glasgow Green in support of the shipyard workers of the Upper Clyde. Music, colourful banners, cheering crowds and warm weather gave the event a carnival atmosphere. The great assembly arrived at the Green where they were addressed by leading politicians and trade unionists, including Tony Benn and Willie Ross. However, it was the local workers leader, Jimmy Reid, whose defiant oratory brought the most jubilant and raucous response from the great crowd thronging the Green.

To some extent of course, preaching and political speechifying are performance. However, from early on, Glasgow Green also drew all manner of ballad bawlers, tumblers, cure peddlers, magicians and novelty acts; and not just during the Glasgow Fair. From the Middle Ages on, the kind of performer who hopes to get paid for it, whether local or touring, made for Glasgow Green.

Demonstration on the Green, 1920s

Glasgow Fair, *John Knox, c. 1832*

The Green has long been a venue for popular entertainment. Every weekend the local citizens would throng its western edge seeking diversion and amusements from the cranks, quacks, turns and spouters. For verve and variety, the nineteenth century was probably the Green's heyday as a site for spectacle and entertainment. One did not need to visit the singing salons, precursors of the music halls, for distraction. A ballad on any subject could be commissioned on the spot from Rutherford's 'Penny Geggie', quickness often trumping quality.

Among the characters to be relished during those promenades was the 'Glasgow Homer', Blind Alec. This fiddler and songwriter had a prodigious thirst for whisky. Another notable character, Hirstlin' Kate, propelled herself in a child's cart, singing songs on request. Auld Hawkie, singer, soothsayer and wit, joked with regard to the swelling Irish population that, "we canna' get the use o' our ain jyles fur them!". Jamie Blue, Hawkie's principal rival, got his name from his trade making illegal buttons. Bell Geordie announced the news with rhymes, songs and jokes.

The Calton minister, John Aitken, was a popular al-fresco preacher on the Green, while Rab Ha, the Glasgow glutton, was, as popular eating competitions demonstrated, unvanquishably greedy. Auld Malaber, an Irish 'giant' was a sort of one-man circus. Patrick Feeney – his real name – was usually no drinker but one boozy bout left him unable to catch a steel ball in the cup on his brow, which was his speciality. He carried the scar on his forehead until he died, at the ripe old age, for the time, of 83.

Glasgow Green has continued to be used for performances, pop concerts, recitals at the People's Palace, fireworks displays and children's events. The Green's political credentials are confirmed every May with the continuing celebration of the first day of that month. Virtually every year since the declaration of 1 May as an international working-class holiday in 1889, the Green has hosted gatherings and speeches.

The Green's role as a focus for religious gatherings also endures. In July 1982 the missionary, Mother Teresa of Calcutta, addressed a rally at the Green organised by the Society for the Protection of Unborn Children. However, despite the continuance of preaching and public throng, the Green is not, perhaps, quite the place of protest and politics it was in the times of Wesley, Auld Hawkie and John MacLean.

The Collins Fountain, c. 1900

FOUR

Drink, Death and the Monument

IN 1842, THE GREAT IRISH temperance campaigner, Father Theobald Mathew, arrived in Glasgow at the invitation of the Western Scottish Temperance Union to address a rally at Glasgow Green. To a large crowd he thundered against the evils of drink. This charismatic preacher led an international temperance movement, named the Knights of Father Mathew in his honour. In response to the good Father's exhortations, a large number of Glaswegians took the pledge of total abstinence, joining the estimated seven million worldwide whom he persuaded to sign up. However, the Irish 'Apostle of Temperance' was far from the first to preach the cause of abstinence at Glasgow Green.

In the early nineteenth century, the city's huge drink problem had resulted in the founding of a number of organisations, most notably the Glasgow and West of Scotland Temperance Society, whose leading members were John Dunlop and the publisher William Collins. The latter produced handbills and pamphlets in the cause. While his print business had started out producing bibles and other religious literature, it grew steadily under his guidance and that of his son, also William. In time, William Collins the Younger would become Glasgow's Lord Provost (1877-1880), be honoured with a Knighthood and be recognised by his fellow temperance reformers with the erection of a fountain at Glasgow Green bearing his name.

The fight for temperance and marches and rallies in its cause were a consistent feature of Glasgow Green's life throughout the nineteenth century. However, the early years of the century were marked by a much more vociferous and heated protest that the government regarded as a real threat. The roots of the unrest, which, in time, would become known as the Radical War, can be traced to the end of the previous century. The principles of freedom, which had underpinned the French Revolution, and notions of equality, propounded by writers including Robert Burns and Tom Paine, became the subject of much debate, encouraged by pamphleteers and the inspiring rhetoric of a large number of activists.

The unrest which characterised this era was partly in response to the economic downturn after the Napoleonic wars, partly a realisation that, in America and France, new systems of government had been established on egalitarian principles. The reform of parliament, the right to vote, poverty and unemployment became the driving forces of widespread discontent.

Alarmed by the growing threat of revolt, the government established a network of agents and informers who actively encouraged agitation for reform. Through its spies, the government learned of plans to restore the Scottish Parliament and declare independence from England. In April 1820, a proclamation was published demanding freedom for the Scots and around 60,000 workers supported a weavers strike throughout central Scotland. In the days that followed, marches set out from Glasgow and Strathaven. These marches were broken up by the military, a process

Temperance rally, c. 1910

that led to further unrest including eight deaths in Greenock when a mob attacked the militia who opened fire.

Eighty-eight marchers were charged with treason, including James (Pearlie) Wilson from Strathaven. Wilson, credited with the redesign of the stocking frame on which the purl stitch was used to eliminate the need for a seam (hence his nickname), had been politically active since 1792, a passionate advocate for workers rights.

Despite pleas for clemency, Wilson was found guilty of High Treason and sentenced to be hung, beheaded and quartered. His execution was carried out before a crowd of 20,000 at Glasgow Green on Wednesday 30 August 1820. His last words were reported as, "Did you ever see such a crowd, Thomas?". Whether in response to the mood of the crowd, out of respect for the dignity of his victim or, perhaps, through loss of nerve, the executioner – a twenty-year-old medical student – left Wilson's body unmutilated. Two of Wilson's fellow Radicals were executed at Stirling and twenty others had sentences of death commuted to transportation to New South Wales.

'Facing the Monument'

For most of those who were hanged at Jocelin Square, meeting their end in sight of Nelson's Monument was an ignominious fate. Indeed in recognition of the view from the scaffold, the term 'facing the Monument' became a popular Glasgow metaphor for the disgrace of death by hanging. In Pearlie Wilson's case, however, his brutal end raised him to the status of a minor martyr. Within hours of his death, his body was dug up and taken back to his home town of Strathaven by his daughter and a niece.

Ironically, the monument erected to Pearlie Wilson in Strathaven, by public subscription in 1846, is in the form of an Egyptian obelisk. Although on a more modest scale, this was the same style of monument as that to Admiral Lord Nelson at Glasgow Green, the last sight Wilson beheld on earth. The inscription commends him as 'a patriotic Scotsman' and praises him for his endeavours towards progress and reform,

"By the adoption of which Great Britain has secured domestic peace and consolidated her power among the nations".

The inscription avoids mention of the fact that Wilson died in the cause of independence for Scotland. The lack of any reference to his execution is, perhaps, an understandable rewriting of history. However, the memorial at least acknowledges the sacrifice of one of Scotland's most notable martyrs in the cause of free speech.

Others who were executed at Glasgow Green may have been a little more deserving of their fate. However, a list published in 1820 of hangings at Glasgow over the previous six decades cites only twelve out of sixty-four executions being for the crime of murder. The remainder were variously for robbery, theft, housebreaking, forgery and of course one, that of Pearlie Wilson, for high treason. In 1800, Peter Gray was hung for 'hamesucken', an archaic Scottish legal term for breaking into someone's home with the intention of committing assault. Another unusual charge, resulted in the cotton spinner, Hugh Kennedy, being hanged in 1834. His crime was throwing vitriol (sulphuric acid) during a workers rally.

The last man to be publicly hanged in Glasgow was Dr. Edward Pritchard. By 8am on 28 July 1865, a crowd estimated at over 80,000 had gathered at Jocelin Square. Pritchard's crimes had been widely reported and his professional standing raised huge public interest. Reporting his trial in Edinburgh *The Scotsman* newspaper recorded that,

"He is a tall, stout, well-built man, rather prepossessing and with sharply defined features".

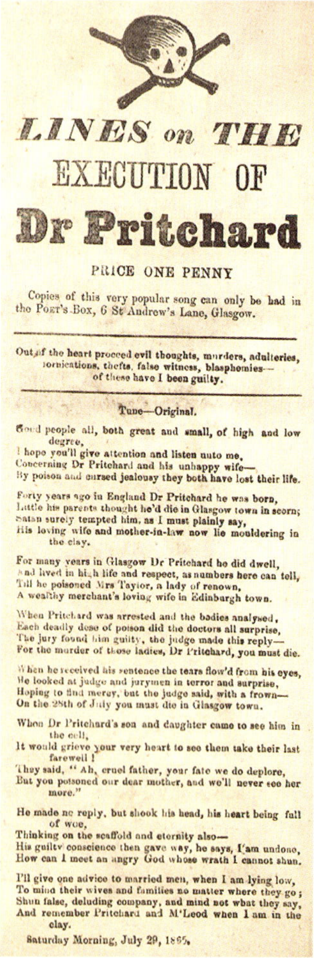

LINES on THE EXECUTION OF

Dr Pritchard

PRICE ONE PENNY

Copies of this very popular song can only be had in the Poet's Box, 6 St Andrew's Lane, Glasgow.

Out of the heart proceed evil thoughts, murders, adulteries, fornications, thefts, false witness, blasphemies— of these have I been guilty.

Tune—Original.

Good people all, both great and small, of high and low degree,
I hope you'll give attention and listen unto me,
Concerning Dr Pritchard and his unhappy wife—
By poison and cursed jealousy they both have lost their life.

Forty years ago in England Dr Pritchard he was born,
Little his parents thought he'd die in Glasgow town in scorn;
Satan surely tempted him, as I must plainly say,
His loving wife and mother-in-law now lie mouldering in the clay.

For many years in Glasgow Dr Pritchard he did dwell,
And lived in high life and respect, as numbers here can tell,
Till he poisoned Mrs Taylor, a lady of renown,
A wealthy merchant's loving wife in Edinburgh town.

When Pritchard was arrested and the bodies analysed,
Each deadly dose of poison did the doctors all surprise,
The jury found him guilty, the judge made this reply—
For the murder of those ladies, Dr Pritchard, you must die.

When he received his sentence the tears flow'd from his eyes,
He looked at judge and jurymen in terror and surprise,
Hoping to find mercy, but the judge said, with a frown—
On the 28th of July you must die in Glasgow town.

When Dr Pritchard's son and daughter came to see him in the cell,
It would grieve your very heart to see them take their last farewell!
They said, "Ah, cruel father, your fate we do deplore,
But you poisoned our dear mother, and we'll never see her more."

He made no reply, but shook his head, his heart being full of woe,
Thinking on the scaffold and eternity also—
His guilty conscience then gave way, he says, I'am undone,
How can I meet an angry God whose wrath I cannot shun.

I'll give one advice to married men, when I am lying low,
To mind their wives and families no matter where they go;
Shun false, deluding company, and mind not what they say,
And remember Pritchard and M'Leod when I am in the clay.

Saturday Morning, July 29, 1865.

The Scotsman continued that, in court,

> *"His manner is that of a well-bred man who has been accustomed to mingle a good deal in society. The expression of his countenance during the day was sad and thoughtful and he seemed cool and collected".* [12]

Yet this was a man with a murky past being tried on two counts of murder by poisoning. He was having an affair with a fifteen-year-old servant, Mary MacLeod. The prosecution gave his wife's discovery of his adultery as a credible motive for his crimes. The indictment, as quoted in *The Scotsman*, was that he,

> *"Did wickedly and feloniously administer to, or cause to be taken by,*

12 *The Scotsman*, Tuesday 4 July 1895 p5

Mary Jane Taylor or Pritchard, now deceased, your wife, and then residing with you, in egg-flip and in cheese, and in porter or beer and in wine… or in some medicine… tartarised antimony and aconite… or some other poison or poisons".

Pritchard was also charged with varying the recipe by administering poison to his mother-in-law,

"In tapioca and in porter or beer, and in a medicine called Battley's Sedative Solution…" [13]

The jury in Edinburgh High Court did not take long to deliver their verdict of guilty on both charges.

Those condemned to hang at Glasgow Green spent their last few hours with only a slop bucket and a wooden stool for company in an underground cell in the Justiciary Courts at the Saltmarket. When the time came for Dr. Pritchard's execution, the normal nicety of drawing across a curtain below the scaffold was dispensed with to enable the huge crowd to watch Pritchard's death throes. After his ignominious end Pritchard's body was cut down and taken to be buried under the flagstones in the central courtyard at the Justiciary Courts, with only his initials and the date of his execution as a memorial.

13 *The Scotsman* Ibid

Laundry on the Green c. 1910

FIVE

Love, Literature and Laundry

THE CONNECTIONS BETWEEN LITERATURE, love and laundry in the long history of Glasgow Green go well beyond the merely alliterative. For centuries, the Green was the venue for communal laundry. Just as Tony Roper's play, *The Steamie*, uses the wash-house to celebrate romance amidst the tenement life of the 1950s, there is no doubt that many an amorous alliance blossomed among the fluttering petticoats on the Green's shared washing lines and amid the linens laid out on the grass to bleach in the sun.

Glasgow's 'other river', the Kelvin, is celebrated in the mid-nineteenth century evocation of how 'The Bleacher Lass O' Kelvinhaugh' won a young man's heart as she scrubbed and rinsed. Going by this example of romantic verse it certainly seems that there's love and literature in washing one's dirty linens in public! There is no doubt that Glasgow Green, in addition to its rich history as a communal washing ground, has always furnished inspiration, recuperation and a setting for writers.

Glasgow's first Poet-Laureate, Edwin Morgan, has written memorably about the city and its Green. In his poem *Colloquy in*

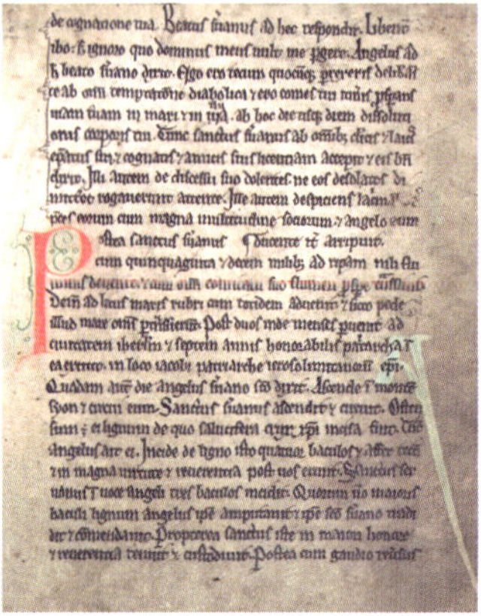

Page from Jocelin's manuscript of the Life of Kentigern (Mungo), c. 1180

Glaschu, he draws on the life of St. Mungo written by the monk Jocelin of Furness in the late twelfth century. Morgan's verses suggest that, in the sixth century, Mungo and Columba chanted stanzas back and forth during the latter's fraternal visit to Glasgow. While the tale of Columba's visit may be fanciful, there was certainly a well-established tradition of monastic poetry and writing, much of it celebrating the lives of saints. St. Columba's reputation as a composer of verses was widely reported.

Nearly a millennium later and in a much more belligerent tone, Blind Harry's epic poem *The Wallace* (c. 1477) – which became the source for much of Mel Gibson's *Braveheart* – features a battle with the English on the High Street, a slingshot from the Green.

From the mid-fifteenth century and for over four centuries onwards, Glasgow University occupied its original site on the High Street. This august seat of learning was a brisk five minutes walk from the Green. Alas there is no record of early poetry produced by the staff and students. There is no question however that the quiet contemplation of the Green and the escape from study found in the many taverns of the area must have spawned contributions to the ongoing anthology of Glasgow stories, poetry and songs.

While there is little evidence of early Glasgow poetry, Hamish Whyte's important anthology, *Mungo's Tongues*, suggests that, by the late seventeenth century, Glasgow's poets had attained real mastery.

The Green and its environs became a popular focus for Glasgow's writers from around 1630. Written in Latin, Arthur Johnston's *Glasguh* describes a veritable Parnassus between the Molendinar and the Clyde. John Barclay's *Glasgow* of 1685 is also rich in comparisons with antiquity. He is particularly full of praise for the "Bridge of Pollisht Stone", which guarantees to "travellers o'er Clyde a Passage safe".

It was very much the fashion of the time to describe the city and the Green, its principle public space, as being wonders of the world, worthy of the ancient Greek gods:

> *"Its Northern Bank a lovely Green displays*
> *Who's every Prospect fresh Delights conveys",*

rhapsodised James Arbuckle in his poem *Glotta* in 1721. Fifteen years later the first full-length book on the city, John M'Ure's *The History of Glasgow*, portrays "the most beautiful city of the world", poised 'deliciously' on the banks of the Clyde. The enthusiasm and delight of these early chronicles is notable, though some of their sentiments may be a little implausible – and nobody mentions the rain!

The Green's first real poetic maestro was the radical Bridgeton weaver, John Mayne. His poetry sets forth, with an honesty verging on the treasonable, his pro-Labour and anti-monarchist views. For Mayne, Glasgow Green was both a subject for his verse and the venue for demonstrations against the social ills of the age. He did find time to admire some of the finer prospects offered by Glasgow's leisure grounds, particularly its views of the female form,

> *"Whae'er has Danered out at e'een,*
> *And seen the sights that I hey seen!*
> *For strappan Ladies typed and clean,*

Scotch Washing, illustration from a snuff box

May safely tell,
That search the kintra Glasgow Green,
Will bare the belle". 14

It could well be that the Bard himself relished similar visions of femininity. Robert Burns was in Glasgow seldom but, lodging as he did at the Black Bull Inn (now the site of a branch of Marks and Spencer on Argyle Street), he would surely have sought recreation, and maybe a peek at the laundry lasses, on the nearby Green.

Before ever she met him, Burns' 'Clarinda', Nancy McElhose, may have dreamed of someone just like him on her walks through the Green, so close to her home in the Saltmarket. Much later, in the 1990s, one of the most renowned twentieth century devotees of the Bard, John Cairney, would recall the poet's adoration of his

14 "Glasgow, A Poem, 1783" *Mungo's Tongues* p35.

muse, Nancy, in the Burns cabaret he created for one of Glasgow's most intimate and memorable venues, the Inn on the Green.

Another East End inn, the Saracen's Head, features in many historic accounts. Coaches from London and other points south used to arrive at the Saracen's Head as one of their first ports of call in Glasgow. It was there that the Wordsworths, William and Dorothy, put up in August 1803. On Tuesday 23 August, they took a walk across the Green. At the bleaching ground they witnessed the washerwomen tramping linens in their great tubs. From the Wordsworths' slightly snooty perspective these poor women, whom they surmised would usually be happy, were made 'stupid and cheerless' by the miserable wet weather which prevailed on their visit. In the washhouse, they guestimated, were to be found one, two or even three hundred women, whom they pronounced, 'civil'.

A great friend and admirer of William Wordsworth was the Glasgow-born poet John Wilson. Of all those who have joined the themes of love and laundry at Glasgow Green, the so-called Laureate of the Clyde was undoubtedly the most lyrical:

"Here barefoot beauties lightly trip along;
Their snowy labours all the verdure throng;
The Linen some with rosy fingers rub,
And the white foam o'er flows the smoking tub;
Her polished feet another nimbly plies,
Their bright approach impurity refines;
At every touch the linen brighter shines,
Whether they bathe it in the crystal wave,
Or on the stream the whitening surges lave,
Or from the painted can the fountain pour,
Softly descending in a shining shower,

Washing on the Green, c. 1910

> *Till, as it lies, its fair transparent hue,*
> *Shows like a lily dipt in morning dew".* [15]

There is no more romanticised view of the labours of the Glasgow washerwomen. However, Wilson's verse is also vividly descriptive of the age-old process of washing linen out-of-doors at Glasgow Green.

In 1823, another Glasgow poet who chose to sign himself, cryptically, as WB, produced verses in praise of the city, depicting the

15 John Wilson, quoted in Thomas Fairbairn, *Relics of Ancient Architecture and other Picturesque Scenes in Glasgow* (Glasgow, 1849)

Clyde as a "gorgeous Eastern Queen". In his poem, Queen is rhymed with 'vernal Green', hymning this historic part of the city. After some hesitation – "but where shall I begin?" – his poem, *Glasgow*, starts with the Green itself, doubtless reflecting its well established role as the gathering and event space for all of Glasgow's citizens.

In his invaluable *Glasgow Encyclopædia*, Joe Fisher adds the achievements of the dissipated peddler poet, James Macfarlane, to those of John Mayne. Fisher also holds the works of Alexander Rodger and Alexander Smith in high esteem. The output of this quartet of Glasgow poets straddles the seventeenth and eighteenth centuries.

Alexander Smith's masterpiece, like so many other poems of the time, was simply entitled with subject and the date – *Glasgow, 1857*. The poem is ambivalent about the sylvan and pastoral splendours of the Calton and its parkland in the years before the industrial revolution. This writer knows, "the tragic hearts of towns", but can see through the factory smoke, "another beauty, sad and stern". Perhaps his exhausted fellow users of the Green shared his conclusion that,

"A sacredness of love and death,
Dwells in thy noise and smoky breath".

Juggling the city's paradoxes and contradictions has also been a favourite pastime of Edwin Morgan. His unsettling 1960s poem, *Glasgow Green*, abandons the grandiose classical imagery of the area's earlier celebrants in favour of a much more down-to-earth tone. Here,

"A cigarette glows and fades upon a cough"

and

"Meth men mutter on benches,
Pawed by a river fog". [16]

At evening on the Green, "All shadows are alive" as, "The sheets, blow and whip".

The Green has long played a role in Glasgow's prose fiction, a topic brilliantly considered by Moira Burgess in her influential 1986 study, *The Glasgow Novel*. According to Burgess there is scarcely a Glasgow-themed book in which the Green does not feature, from Sarah Tyler's *St Mungo's City* of 1885, through the works of Frederick Niven, Dot Alan, George Blake, Edward Gaitens, James Barke and George Friel. Given its prominence, geographically and symbolically, how could working-class novels of the depression years not ponder upon the Green or have major characters visit the city's oldest park?

Many consider Archie Hind's *The Dear Green Place* (1966) to be *the* Glasgow novel. Its working class hero, the would-be writer Matt, is much given to broody wandering through the city. He turns up,

> *"Past the gates of the Glasgow Green to the parapet of the bridge from where he could see the old Clyde, the colour of a backcourt puddle, winding in through the Green towards the centre of the city".*

In a later series of crime novels, William McIlvanney's *Laidlaw* spends much of his time investigating in the pubs of the Gallowgate – among them the Saracen's Head. There are to be found the gangsters who add their own characteristically East End charisma to McIlvanney's dialogue. Indeed, as these works demonstrate,

16 Edwin Morgan, *Collected Poems*, Manchester 2004

the Green's reputation has veered between the rascally and the respectable down through the centuries.

Alasdair Gray's Frankensteinesque *Poor Things* (1992) has its heroine jump from the suspension bridge at the Green. Her suicide is witnessed by the Humane Society officer, Geddes, who in the novel's account has "a small morgue attached to his dwelling". Bella's tragic end is all the more poignant in the light of her doomed love story.

The author and television presenter Bill Knox set his last novel, *The Lazarus Widow*, around Glasgow Green and the Clyde. While the novel's structure is that of a crime thriller, its setting is powerfully evoked. Among its characters is an Officer of the Glasgow Humane Society, heroically depicted.

There were many ballad criers around the Green, the most renowned being William 'Hawkie' Cameron who had a jealous rival in 'Jamie Blue' McIndoe. In one famous hawking contest, Cameron emerged the victor by far, proving either the superior quality of his verse or that his was much the louder voice!

Following in this long tradition of folk verse, Glasgow's East End was also home to two of Britain' foremost twentieth century poetic songwriters, Matt McGinn and Adam McNaughtan. Indeed, McGinn's ashes were scattered on the Green in 1977 (or, rather, half of them, the other portion being spread upon the gravesite of the socialist leader John MacLean at Eastwood).

McNaughtan adapted *Airn John*, a powerful piece of invective, written to prevent the users of the Green (mainly poor) being taxed to pay for those who patronised the nascent Kelvingrove Park (mostly rich). The original ballad that inspired McNaughtan came from 'The Poet's Box'. This vendor of rather high quality topical doggerel – 'The Grand Temple of the Muse!' – also sold cakes of soap bearing lovers' charms and laces, a penny a dozen, from a shop in St Andrew's Lane. McNaughtan's reworking of this historic verse lent his (in every sense) powerful voice to the campaign to prevent a motorway being routed through the Green.

Hugh MacDonald would certainly have approved of efforts to preserve the Green for pedestrians. To this eminent Victorian journalist can be attributed the beginnings of the ramblers movement in the west of Scotland. His vastly influential publication, *Rambles Round Glasgow,* is just one of the many achievements commemorated by the memorial fountain that stands as a solid reminder of the Green's greatest historical chronicler.

As MacDonald observed, the Green had no shortage of trysting spots for luckier lovers. It certainly provided welcome, if slightly al-fresco, 'privacy' for the many 'braw wooers' crowded into the district's teeming, overcrowded tenements. 'Arn's Well' (named for the arn or alder trees which shaded it) was especially popular. As MacDonald pointed out, with reference to the adjoining bleaching green:

> *'The character of a sweetheart... may be learned more effectually there than either at kirk or market'.* [17]

In 1756, a series of serpentine paths were provided. These alas proved too popular as lovers' lanes and, after public outcry, were eventually replaced.

MacDonald also relates how marriage minded maidens, having picked 'the mystic yarrow' by the banks of the Clyde on the evening of 30 April, would secrete these clusters of white flowers beneath their pillows. Awakening on Mayday morning, they would seek, in shadow or silhouette, the figure of their husbands to be. One

17 Hugh MacDonald, *Rambles Round Glasgow in the 1850s:* The Public Green (Glasgow 1910, reprinted Blanefield, 1982)

Hugh MacDonald, 1817-1860 painted by A S Mackay

Dublin colleen, trusting to the magical properties of yarrow blooms, is reputed to have lilted:

'As Joseph dreamed of Mary,
And took her for his bride,
So in dream I wish to see,
My true love by my side'. [18]

Over the centuries, whichever of Glasgow Green's many amorous opportunities the love-lorn decided to pursue, one thing was certain – if things didn't work out there was always the washhouse to wring out that tear-stained hanky!

18 Hugh MacDonald, *ibid*

Opening ceremony of the People's Palace, 1898

Glasgow Orpheus Choir concert in the Winter Gardens, c. 1910

SIX

Palaces, Monuments and Plashing Fountains

THE 136 ACRES OF Glasgow's central park are bounded by some of the city's finest historic buildings and punctuated by a number of remarkable monuments. The rolling landscape of the Green itself features two palaces, no less than four fountains and a triumphal arch.

As its name suggests, the People's Palace tells Glasgow's story. In the words of its former curator Elspeth King,

> *"There is no museum, gallery, arts or community centre quite like it anywhere else in the world".* [19]

The aspiration to create a museum for the East End of Glasgow goes back to the 1860s when the sale of the old Bridgeton Bleaching Green raised £2,500, which was invested to fund such an endeavour. However, it wasn't until April 1895, supported by an additional £18,000 from the Caledonian Railway Company, that work started on A.B. McDonald's French Renaissance-style creation.

19 Elspeth King, *The People's Palace and Glasgow Green* (Edinburgh, 1991)

The People's Palace, c.1910

The museum, north-facing in orange Dumfriesshire sandstone, is richly embellished with symbolic sculptures by William Kellock Brown. On its main façade draped female figures represent shipbuilding, mathematics, sculpture, painting, engineering and textile manufacturing. Above these, statues representing science and art are set on plinths flanking the central figure, representing progress, which stands proudly in front of the building's great dome.

On show within the People's Palace is an extraordinarily diverse collection of objects commemorating many of the events in Glasgow's long and colourful history alongside displays depicting social history, industry and culture. This large and impressive collection ensures that the building fulfils the promise set out for it in Lord Rosebery's address at the opening ceremony on 22 January 1898. He hoped that the building would be become,

The Winter Gardens

> *"A palace of pleasure and imagination around which the people may place their affections and which may give them a home on which their memory may rest".* [20]

Extending behind the People's Palace, its spectacular conservatory, the Winter Gardens, originally designed as a venue for musical performance, is now home to a popular café and a regular venue for parties and weddings. Constructed by Boyd & Son of Paisley, this huge, wrought-iron, cast-iron and glass enclosure was, according to popular tradition, designed to emulate the hull of Lord Nelson's flagship, *Victory*. Sadly, the story, though much repeated, doesn't stand close scrutiny.

In 1998, the Winter Gardens was badly damaged by fire. Superbly restored, it serves as a magnificent adjunct to the People's

20 Lord Rosebery, quoted in People's Palace leaflet

Collapsed Templeton's factory, November 1889

Templeton's Carpet Factory, c. 1910

Palace, a unique venue for events and each year welcomes thousands of visitors to enjoy its café.

Close to the People's Palace, on the edge of the Green, sits the office block of the former Templeton's Carpet Factory. In crimson brick, terracotta, brilliant glazing and colourful enamel mosaic, the building was modelled on the Doge's Palace in Venice. The architect, William Leiper, was asked by his client to produce a work in emulation of the Venetian masterpiece, which James Templeton considered the finest building he had ever seen.

Leiper's achievement is undoubtedly a brilliant visual triumph. However, this joyous façade, vividly reflecting the carpets that were manufactured in the sheds behind, also marks the scene of one of the worst tragedies in Glasgow's industrial history. On the night of 1 November 1889, a fierce storm destroyed the partially built façade of Leiper's building. It collapsed onto the carpet sheds behind, killing twenty-nine women and girls. It seems extraordinary in

Templeton's workers; Jacquard looms; the building today

retrospect that a re-engineered version of the same building was instructed soon after. The reconstructed Doge's Palace opened in 1892.

After the demise of carpet manufacturing at Glasgow Green, Charles Robertson & Partners restored and converted the various buildings around the Templeton Factory's central courtyard to a business centre for the Scottish Development Agency in the early 1980s. More recently the site has become the focus of a new initiative which will see this remarkable group of buildings converted to housing, incorporating 175 apartments housed within the existing buildings and a dramatic, new, balconied block facing the Green. The masterplan for this ambitious endeavour is by ZM Architecture.

The Templeton Factory is the most colourful building in Glasgow, and undoubtedly the most ostentatious in the environs of the Green. However the periphery of Glasgow's largest park features a whole series of distinguished buildings, each of which has its own tale to tell of Glasgow's economic, social and architectural history.

Former Greenview School

Almost at the eastern extremity of the Green, the great Glasgow architect and entrepreneur, Charles Wilson, designed the former Greenview School in the form of a little Italian palazzo. Dating from 1846, the building was originally Greenhead House, subsequently the Buchanan Institute for Destitute Children and then, through most of the twentieth century, served as the aptly named school. The building was extended in 1873, when the larger than life-size sandstone figure *Young Scholar* was added. Sculpted by William Brodie, the figure sits deep in thought, presumably puzzling over the answer to a complex problem on the slate balanced on his left knee.

Closer to the city centre, and also inspired by Italian precedents, sits the last of what was once a magnificent row of houses on Charlotte Street. Dating from the late eighteenth century, 52 Charlotte Street was converted in the late 1980s by Nicholas Groves-Raines Architects as six flats for rent for the National Trust for Scotland.

At the southern end of the same row once stood David Dale's magnificent mansion house, designed by one of the most distinguished and best known of all Scottish architects, Robert Adam. Sadly, this building was demolished in 1954 to be replaced by the extension for Our Lady and St. Francis School. This boldly modern composition in concrete, blue engineering-brick and glass, dates from 1964. It was designed by arguably the most important Scottish architectural practice of the post World War II era, Gillespie, Kidd & Coia. The school closed in 1989 and, while its main range was subsequently demolished, the southern extension is now occupied by the Wise Group.

While the site of David Dale's house is now occupied by an important mid-twentieth century building, his garden and much of the landscape around it is home to the predominantly white-

Homes for the Future

style, late twentieth century, Homes for the Future. Created to mark Glasgow's year as UK City of Architecture in 1999, this development incorporates work by notable Glasgow, UK and international architects. The copper building at the development's eastern edge is by Ian Ritchie Architects while its neighbours along Greendyke Street are variously by Ushida Findlay from Tokyo, the Londoner Rick Mather and Elder & Cannon. The development behind includes work by McKeown Alexander, RMJM and Wren Rutherford Architects.

Also now serving as housing is Homes for the Future's neighbour, the former Hide, Wool and Tallow Auction Market by John Keppie (1890). This four storey, red sandstone building is a survivor from an era when this whole area was a rich mix of impressive warehouse buildings pressed around with traditional tenemental housing, most of it long since demolished. Following the lead of Homes for the Future and nearby St. Andrew's Square, and acknowledging the trend towards housing, this great warehouse was also converted to flats as the twentieth century came to its close.

On the corner of Greendyke Street and Turnbull Street, the little St. Andrew-by-the-Green is Scotland's oldest surviving Episcopal church building. Like its near neighbour and namesake, St. Andrew's-in-the-Square, this composition is classically inspired; however, the scale here is that of a Palladian Veneto mansion house rather than that great temple of classicism, complete with its lordly tower, created by Allan Dreghorn and Mungo Nasmith.

While symbols of faith and places of worship played a major part in the lives of eighteenth and nineteenth century Glaswegians, the environs of the Green were also the focus of much of the city's leisure. In addition to the proliferation of pubs and shebeens, the nineteenth century saw the rapid growth of theatres and circuses. Mumford's 'Penny Geggie', one of many similar emporia, occupied a site at the end of Greendyke Street close to Saltmarket, offering, as its name suggests, short melodramas and abbreviated versions of the works of Shakespeare and other dramatic classics at a penny a time.

Former Mumford's Theatre, c. 1900

In 1845, John Henry Anderson, a former conjurer known as 'The Wizard of the North' built the imposing, classically fronted, City Theatre, which had a capacity of 5,000. Cooke's Circus sat close-by. Both buildings were relatively short lived, Anderson's theatre burning down just five months after it opened and Cooke's being destroyed by fire only two weeks later, in December 1845.

Justiciary Courthouse

The Green may well have been a focus for entertainment and revelry, but the Justiciary Courthouse by William Stark (1814) sits nearby, a powerful, classical symbol of the authority of the Courts, sending out the stern message that the law is close by, ready to step in if things get out of hand. Originally designed to serve as courts, municipal offices and a jail, Stark's competition-winning, Greek revival design was converted to serve as courts alone in 1913. The arrival of this building also saw the shifting of public executions from their former site at Glasgow Cross to Jocelin (or Jail) Square. Between 1814 and 1865, seventy-one people (sixty-seven men and four women) were hanged at Glasgow Green 'facing the monument'.

Happily, the view from the Justiciary Courthouse has long since lost its gibbet and, instead, is focused upon the extraordinary McLennan Arch, Glasgow's most peripatetic work of architecture. The arch was originally the centrepiece of the magnificent frontage of Robert and James Adam's sumptuous Assembly Rooms on Ingram Street (1792). However, at the instigation of Bailie James McLennan, it was reconstructed at the junction of Greendyke

McLennan Arch

Street and Monteith Row in 1894 when the Assembly Rooms were demolished to enable the extension of the General Post Office. In 1922, the arch was moved once again, this time to the end of Charlotte Street. Since 1991, it has occupied what is, hopefully, its final site as the magnificent gateway to Glasgow Green. It is reminiscent of the triumphal arches of ancient Rome and, appropriately, features classical reliefs of Apollo and the Three Graces.

The southern edge of the Green is delineated by the river Clyde. The importance of the river to this area and local leisure is marked by two boathouses. The west boathouse was created for the Clyde and Clydesdale Amateur Rowing Club. Built in 1905 by Glasgow Corporation, its timber-framed construction is unusual for Scotland. The east boathouse was built in 1933.

Set between the two boathouses, the dainty St. Andrew's Suspension Bridge was built by the engineer Neil Robson in 1854.

Suspension Bridge; Humane Society House, early 19th century

Its classical portals were witness to well over a century of workers crossing from the overcrowded Gorbals to their daily tasks in the city; women, borne down by the burden of linens, en-route to the washhouses and drying greens at Glasgow Green itself; and children heading for school. More recently, the bridge has connected the revitalised Gorbals, massively regenerated since the advent of the Crown Street Masterplan in the early 1990s, to the leisure and events of Glasgow Green and, via the Green, to the attractions of the city centre.

Close to the Suspension Bridge stands the Glasgow Humane Society house. Established for the purpose of rescuing persons drowning in the Clyde, the Humane Society celebrated its 200th birthday in 1990. The current house replaces one built shortly after the founding of the Society and demolished in the 1930s.

Close to the Humane Society's house stands the extraordinary Nelson Monument. This obelisk, commemorating the Vice Admiral's victories was created to mark:

"The loss of a hero whose name will be immortal and his memory ever dear to his country". [21]

Such was the admiration of Glaswegians for Britain's greatest naval hero that, within nine months of his death, they raised the huge sum of £2,075 to commission David Hamilton, the city's most renowned architect, to create the first monument to Nelson raised by public subscription. Completed in 1806, the mighty sandstone obelisk, 44m high, was inspired by the carved columns marking the entrances to ancient Egyptian temples. Yet on 5 August 1810, in a violent storm, it was struck by lightning. The top five metres collapsed and a military guard kept the public at a safe distance.

21 Admiral Lord Collingwood's Wednesday 6 November 1805 despatch about the Battle of Trafalgar

Nelson's Monument struck by Lightning, *John Knox, c. 1810*

Nelson's Monument, restored 2005

On a visit to Glasgow in 1771, the great American statesman and scientist, Benjamin Franklin, had lectured on the use of lightning conductors for tall buildings. A year later, a 'thunder rod' was attached to the tower of the University on the High Street. The 1810 storm taught Glasgow's citizens a further lesson. When Nelson's Monument was repaired a rod was fitted, keeping the structure safe from lightning strikes for all time to come.

By the 1990s Nelson's Monument was showing its age. Some of its sandstone blocks had fractured and others had eroded. Remarkably, a little elder tree had even taken root at the very apex of the monument. The restoration of the structure required the replacement of damaged stone in matching sandstone. The tenacious elder was removed and the top of the structure was rebuilt. The setting of the monument is now enhanced with new lighting and interpretation, all achieved in time for the Nelson bi-centenary celebrations in October 2005.

While the monument to Nelson is by far the most prominent of the Green's commemorative monuments, there are several others, all much more low key. The Collins Fountain (1881) was created while the younger William Collins was still very much alive and is as much a monument to the temperance movement as to one of its greatest advocates. The Martin Fountain (1894), a memorial to Bailie James Martin, is an ornate cast-iron affair manufactured by Walter McFarlane & Company, whose foundry at Possilpark exported throughout the world. Both the Collins and Martin Fountains were re-sited during the Glasgow Green Renewal Project. The squat memorial construction to Hugh MacDonald was moved to the Green from Gleniffer Braes, Paisley, in 1880, a very solid monument to one of Glasgow's greatest journalists.

Within the garden enclosure at the Winter Gardens stands the statue of James Watt by Grassby, superbly restored, complete with its new head. Also within the Winter Gardens enclosure, Thomas

Martin Fountain; Scultpural railings by Adrian Wiszniewski

Clapperton's bronze sculpture of *Spring-time*, from 1949, has been reunited with its plinth. Clapperton's statue had long since been moved inside the Winter Gardens for safe keeping while its empty plinth bemused many visitors to McPhun's Park. Happily, now that both are reunited, the allegorical subject of the statue explains the relief frieze on the pedestal of children at play. Ironically, many Glaswegians still insist on referring to this sculpture, erroneously, as 'Peter Pan', perhaps on account of a passing resemblance to Sir George Frampton's famous statue of J.M. Barrie's eponymous hero.

A further notable work in the Glasgow Green gallery is Adrian Wiszniewski's impressive sculptural railings at David Dale's Gate (at the foot of Charlotte Street). Wiszniewski's work was the result of a competition judged by, among others, local resident Eleanor McAllister, writer Liz Lochhead and Councillor Aileen Colleran. The competition sought designs that would "reinforce the identity of the Green, reflect the revival in the area and serve as a new landmark in this key Glasgow location". Wiszniewski's frieze, installed in May

2004, depicts a series of faces representing the people of Glasgow in all their diversity. His subject could hardly be more appropriate for Glasgow Green.

Figurative sculpture, in a much more traditional style than that employed by Adrian Wiszniewski, features spectacularly in the most important monument at Glasgow Green, the superbly restored Doulton Fountain.

Originally gifted to Glasgow for the International Exhibition of 1888 in Kelvingrove Park, the Doulton Fountain is the largest terracotta fountain in the world. Marking the substantial input of the Doulton firm to Glasgow's new City Chambers, the fountain reflected the might of both the British Empire and Sir Henry Doulton's company.

Designed by A.E. Pearce and modelled by W. Silver Frith in the, fashionably lavish, French, Ecole des Beaux Arts style, the fountain features four groups of figures, representing India, Canada, South Africa and Australia. Above these is a tier of three soldiers and a sailor representing Scotland, England, Wales and Ireland and,

Doulton Fountain, c.1890

Doulton Fountain today

above these, four female water-bearers clad in flowing gowns. On the very top, symbolically surveying her dominions, stands Queen Victoria bearing orb and sceptre, symbols of imperial power. The Queen was reported to be particularly impressed by the fountain when she visited the Exhibition on 22nd August 1888.

After the Exhibition, there was some debate on relocating the fountain from its temporary site at Kelvingrove (just behind the site now occupied by Kelvingrove Art Gallery and Museum). It was decided that the fountain should become the centrepiece of Glasgow Green. The structure was dismantled and re-erected in 1890.

Unfortunately, lightning struck once again at Glasgow Green and, in 1891, the statue of Queen Victoria, surmounting the fountain, was destroyed. To save cost it was proposed to replace the sculpture with an urn but once again Glasgow benefited from Sir Henry Doulton's generosity and the figure of Queen Victoria, replete with lace, finery and her symbols of power, was replaced in 1892.

For the next seventy years the waters flowed from the urns of the water-bearers and plashed from the imperial lions' heads. But in the 1950s, the fountain's structure started to fail and the water was turned off. The fountain deteriorated rapidly. Fenced off, its cantilevered basin supported by scaffolding and much of its statuary removed for safe-keeping, the fate of the fountain seemed uncertain.

When Glasgow Green's renewal was first mooted, a survey was commissioned to assess the extent of repairs that would be required to restore the magnificent edifice to its former glory. Ibstock Hathernware was commissioned to restore and replace the statuary and moulded detail and Glasgow-based Hunter and Clark to undertake the huge task of dismantling the massive structure and rebuilding the fountain on its new site in front of the People's Palace.

The extraordinary restoration and relocation of the Doulton Fountain cost £3.75m. It incorporates state-of-the-art technology,

Doulton Fountain today

water systems and lighting in a structure restored using unique, custom-designed methods. Acknowledged as the best of its kind in the world, the fountain is revered by experts, loved by those who remember it working in their youth and admired by tourists.

On Monday 9 May 2005 the gloriously restored fountain was ceremonially switched on by Glasgow's Lord Provost, Councillor Liz Cameron. As it splashed back into life a group of local schoolchildren performed a rain dance to celebrate the event.

The restoration of the Doulton Fountain has helped to ensure that the renewed Glasgow Green is a major attraction of world importance. In March 2006, while on a visit to Glasgow, the US Ambassador for the United Kingdom expressly asked to see the restored and relocated Doulton Fountain. In its new setting it is regularly visited by tourist coaches, and the fountain and the Green are now a highlight of the City Sightseeing bus tour itinerary, bringing visitors to the Green four times an hour.

Now the Doulton Fountain, superbly restored, sits as the centrepiece of a new civic setting fronting the People's Palace. Its waters splash once more and, as evening draws on, magical new lighting celebrates the ingenuity and creativity of the Victorians.

SEVEN

Fairs, Football and Fireworks

FOR OVER FIVE CENTURIES, the Green has been Glasgow's gathering place. Its history is a rich pageant of the macabre, of popular culture, sport, political struggle, of religious assemblies and festivities. Throughout the nineteenth century, as Glasgow's industrial growth accelerated and overcrowding became a major problem, the role of the city's parks for recreation became all the more important. Glasgow Green, quite literally, provided a breathing space for countless workers. In his splendid *Glasgow Encyclopædia*, Joe Fisher notes that, on one August day in 1894, more than 78,000 people passed through the gates of Glasgow Green.

While ages past have witnessed rallies, protests and bawdy fairs, more recently marathons, pop concerts, fireworks displays and the World Pipe Band Championships have entertained audiences numbered in tens of thousands.

From very early in its history, the Green has served as a venue for both socialising and sport. Over the years, the Council has responded to local demands and the changing patterns of leisure with provision including a paddling pond near King's Drive that,

Paddling pond, c. 1910

Gymnasium for adults, c. 1900

during the early years of the twentieth century, was a popular haunt for children from far and near.

From 1889, the Sanitary Department took responsibility for creating children's play facilities. Safe, enclosed playgrounds were created with swings, roundabouts and other facilities, supervised by caretakers. The inspiration for this effort came largely from one man, the city's Chief Sanitary Inspector, Peter Fyfe, who was determined that the children of Glasgow's poor families should be given high quality and well-maintained places to play.

While children's play was a major preoccupation of the Council, ensuring that there was adequate provision for adult exercise has also been a continuous theme. In 1860, Mr D.G. Fleming, a Manchester businessman, bequeathed funds to create an adult gymnasium at Glasgow Green as a legacy to his native city. Early photographs show bowler hatted, be-suited gents alongside fellow gymnasts in cloth caps, engaged in strenuous callisthenics. The original gymnasium was built around a substantial wooden frame; however, this was later replaced by the cast-iron frame that still stands, though bereft of the swings, rings and climbing ropes of its heyday.

Other formal provision varied over time. An account of the city, published in 1914, noted that the Green incorporated six bowling greens, two prominently sited just to the west of Nelson's Monument and the rest at the Green's eastern extremity, adjoining Fleshers' Haugh. It also had no less than eighteen football pitches. While the bowling greens are long gone, football is still well served in the form of the Glasgow Green Football Centre. In fact, football in one form or another has been a feature of Glasgow Green, literally for centuries.

Until the early nineteenth century something akin to football took place on the Green every Shrove Tuesday. This annual event had few rules and was open to an unlimited number of players.

Playing football on Fleshers' Haugh, c. 1910

The practice which, by some estimates, extended back over four centuries, was stopped in 1819 with the publication of a by-law prohibiting the playing of

> *"Golf, cricket, shinty, football or any game whatever on the Green of the City".*

Yet football continued to be played on the Green and the Council ultimately introduced formal provision by providing black ash pitches at Fleshers' Haugh. The playing surface was later replaced with red blaes but the change in colour did nothing to improve playing conditions. Innumerable minor injuries were suffered from close contact with the unyielding playing surface at the Green.

Football enthusiasts were undeterred by the quality of the Green's pitches and at Fleshers' Haugh, in 1872, a group from the Clydeside Rowing Club decided that their other sporting passion,

Rangers Football team, c. 1875

for football, justified establishing a team. Thus Rangers Football Club was founded at Glasgow Green where they played for their first three seasons. In 1875, the Club moved to Burnbank off Great Western Road, and the following year to Kinning Park, eventually settling at Ibrox in 1887.

The Green's red blaes pitches continued in use as a venue for both football and, latterly, for the City's annual fireworks display until 1992 when they were closed. In 2000, the Glasgow Green Football Centre opened, offering synthetic and grass pitches for five-a-side, seven-a-side and eleven-a-side football.

Although the founding of Rangers Football Club might be considered the most important historic sporting event at the Green, this rolling landscape also has a distinguished history as a home of golf. In 1760 Glasgow's first known golfer, Patrick Bogle, asked the Council for permission to extend the lodge on the Green for those "who use the exercise of the golf". In 1787, Glasgow Golf Club was

Rowing on the Clyde, c. 1910

founded at the Green. Its twenty-two original members played over a seven hole course with a match constituting of three rounds, or twenty-one holes. Two of the holes in the original course were later named The Monument and The Humane Society, giving a very good idea of their location. In 1792, the golf club applied to the Council to remove the old Herd's House and build a new clubhouse.

The Napoleonic Wars left the golf club much depleted, with many of its members away to fight. Although the club resurfaced between 1809 and 1835, its history records that it was only fully revived in 1870 when it left its first home at the Green for Queen's Park. The Glasgow Golf Club is now based at Killermont and also operates a links course at Irvine.

Although it is not set by the coast, Glasgow Green has the virtue of the next best thing, with the River Clyde flowing on its southern flank. Early nineteenth century depictions of the Green show that, at that time, the river was much wider and that rowing was a popular pastime. Boats were available for hire at Glasgow Green up until the 1970s.

By the 1860s the Council acknowledged the popularity of swimming in the river by providing bathing boxes and springboards at Fleshers' Haugh. Despite lifebelts and the earnest efforts of the Humane Society, however, lives were lost each year and, faced with a mounting death toll and public unease, the Council removed bathing facilities from the Clyde in 1877. The demise of Clyde bathing led to the building of Greenhead Baths. A later plan, to create a lido on the Green, was thwarted by the advent of World War II. The hole that had been dug close to Nelson's Monument was eventually filled in 1948.

While swimming is no longer possible at Glasgow Green, rowing remains an important daily activity. One reason for the continuing popularity of competitive rowing on the Clyde is the presence of the Tidal Weir, which ensures a consistent depth of relatively calm water over the 5000m stretch from the Weir eastward to Westhorn Park, one kilometre beyond Dalmarnock Bridge. In January 1999, a set of *Rules and Guidelines for Rowing on the Clyde* was drawn up and adopted by all the rowing clubs using the river above the Tidal Weir.

The Humane Society, in partnership with the City Council and Strathclyde Police, subsequently published these Rules. In addition to its twenty-two rules and seventeen points of guidance, their booklet incorporates a short history of the Green and an account of the importance of rowing from the early nineteenth century onwards.

The earliest rowing clubs were formed by factory workers or representatives of the various Glasgow trades. Regattas were popular with large crowds gathering on the Green to watch races that, in the early years, were started dramatically by the firing of a cannon.

Through time, university and school clubs evolved. Currently there are fourteen clubs operating on the Clyde and, over a weekend, up to 200 boats can be observed on this stretch of the river. Every year around twenty-four regattas still take place on this section.

Among those who have rowed on the Clyde are both world and Olympic medallists. Another sport in which the Green can legitimately claim a connection with greatness is that of boxing. Benny Lynch, destined to become World Flyweight Champion, honed his craft in his native Gorbals and in the boxing booths that appeared on the Green during the annual fair. After a remarkable early career, Lynch won the Scottish flyweight title in Glasgow at the age of twenty-one. He went on to achieve the world title in Manchester in September 1935. Although he held onto the title for three years and was hailed as one of Glasgow's greatest sons, he was to die in 1946, at the age of only thirty-three, from pneumonia.

Two other sports that are regularly pursued on the Green are those of cycling, using the popular signposted route running parallel with the Clyde, and running. The Green serves as the racing and training venue for Shettleston Harriers. However, it has also been the focus of mass racing for a quarter of a century. Since 1982, the Green has been the finishing point for the Great Scottish Run and its precursor, the Scottish People's Marathon.

Half-marathon finishers, 2001

Funfairs on the Green, John Wright's Chairoplanes (1950s) and today

In its early years, Glasgow's annual race pursued the full, twenty-six mile 385 yards Marathon distance and was, for a time, the third largest marathon in the world, after New York and London. In the late 1980s the complex logistics of organising a full marathon and a growing consensus that thirteen miles was a much healthier distance, prompted a change in the race to designated half-marathon status. The Green still welcomes the runners home to the applause of huge throngs of spectators.

The role of the Green as a leisure ground extends well beyond sporting activity. From the beginning of the nineteenth century until a Council decree in 1870, Glasgow Fair, whose history goes back to medieval times, was an annual feature of Glasgow Green in mid-July. In addition to boxing and gaming booths, Jocelin Square would fill up with canvas tents and wooden booths featuring curiosities, wild beasts and a whole variety of outlandish entertainment, popularly described as 'keek-shows'.

By the late nineteenth century, tolerance for the excesses of the Fair had grown thin and it was temporarily moved away from Glasgow Green. It returned, decades later, significantly modified as a circus and funfair, originally at Fleshers' Haugh and subsequently as simply 'the shows', on a site nearby at the eastern end of the Green.

Live music, very much a feature of the historic Fair, has always played an important part in celebrations and events at the Green. The popularity of open air concerts in the years after the First World War prompted the building of a substantial arena into the sloping site between Nelson's Monument and the river. A large, covered, Art Deco style, bandstand provided an attractive venue for both traditional bands and small orchestras. In the latter part of the twentieth century the building became disused and derelict and the whole site was cleared during improvements to the Green around the period of the renewal of Glasgow's eastern area.

In recent years the popularity of the Green as a gathering space for events and major concerts has grown steadily. On 3 June 1990, the Big Day welcomed more than fifty rock, folk, jazz and classical artists who performed before an estimated crowd of 250,000 at three stages, George Square, Custom House Quay and Glasgow Green. While international performers, like Canadian singer Nancy Griffith, wowed the crowd at the Green, the reception in the early evening for ex-patriate Scot Sheena Easton was a lot less cordial. Her performance started to a cacophony of jeering, but her persistence, humour and determination to keep on singing did win over some of those who had accused her of selling out.

Two years later, on 18 August 1992 (delayed by four days from the date originally published), the greatest pop performer of his generation, Michael Jackson, took to the stage at Glasgow Green before a massive and enthusiastic crowd estimated at over 30,000. Many other equally flamboyant individuals, from Marilyn Manson

Gigs on the Green

to Michael Stipe of REM, have also performed at the Green in recent years. On 22 June 1996, self-declared 'stately homo' Quentin Crisp, addressed a jubilant Pride Scotland rally at the Green.

The Glasgow Green Renewal Project has enhanced the services available to performers and subtly re-engineered the Green's landscape to accommodate performances including major pop concerts and the BBC Proms.

Remember, remember…

Every August the Green is host to one of the biggest noises in the world when the World Pipe Band Championships descends on Glasgow. From early morning until late afternoon, the world's finest exponents of Scotland's national instrument demonstrate their skills. The fact that locally-based musicians are often among the winners testifies to the enduring importance of the piping tradition in the West of Scotland.

The last major event on Glasgow Green's annual calendar is the city's fantastic 5 November fireworks. Over the years, Glasgow's firework displays have achieved huge audience numbers with massive crowds accumulating not only on the Green but also across the Clyde in Gorbals, in neighbouring streets and on high vantage points throughout the city to witness the spectacle. A regular and distinctive feature of Glasgow's displays has been the incorporation of theatrical performances with giant puppets and fire sculptures enhancing the experience for the audience.

On 5 November 2000, a perishingly cold, dry evening, the crowd was welcomed by the traditional warm-up from Radio Clyde featuring DJ's George Bowie and Suzie McGuire. Local singer Josh McGuire (no relation to Suzie) gave a rousing rendition of Ronan Keating's *Life is a Rollercoaster* helping to build the audience, which numbered well over 50,000, to a high pitch of anticipation.

The lights were dimmed and a hush of expectation settled over the crowd. The silence was broken by the mellifluous bass tones of renowned Glasgow actor David Hayman who started to recount the story of Glasgow's own patron saint, St. Mungo. As the tale unfolded, gigantic fire sculptures depicting the elements of the City's crest flared to the accompaniment of a musical track by the young Glasgow composer, David Gilmour. As the story reached its thundering conclusion a huge fire sculpture of Glasgow's crest was raised 100ft over the heads of the crowd. A song by local primary

The Glasgow Show 2005

schoolchildren rang out, and the vibrant, multi-coloured spectacle of the fireworks began.

This is the essence of Glasgow Green. It is a place of history, a place where people gather in protest, in celebration, to witness spectacular events and to tread where fellow Glaswegians have trodden in ages past. This is a landscape formed by history, coloured by events and shaped by the will of the people of Glasgow. This landscape has served Glasgow for centuries and will continue to serve for centuries more, one of the most extraordinary and resonant landscapes on planet earth – the ancient Green of Glasgow!

POSTSCRIPT

Glasgow Green Renewed

THE GLASGOW GREEN RENEWAL PROJECT, completed in 2007, had five principal aims:

- to restore Glasgow Green to its former status as the premier parkland in Glasgow,
- to develop the Green's role as a city park, with particular reference to its unique social importance in the evolution of Glasgow; environmental and education opportunities; active and passive recreation; leisure and the appeal of horticultural excellence,
- to enhance features of heritage importance,
- to achieve a balance between local, city, national and international interests and activities, and
- to achieve excellence in development, management and maintenance.

The masterplan for the Green's renewal followed the design laid-down by James Cleland in the early part of the nineteenth century.

Much that has been achieved is not immediately visible. Debris from air-raid shelters has been removed, contours re-arranged and the ground reinforced to accommodate major events. In addition, however, a number of significant changes have improved every aspect of Glasgow Green's rich and varied landscape:

- boundary treatments – new fencing has replaced the original boundary fences removed in the early 1940s to support the war effort (3.36km of fencing including accurate reproduction heritage fencing along Greendyke Street and Saltmarket and riverside safety fencing edging the Clyde),
- carriageways and paths –surfaces, edging, drainage, lighting, seating and litter bins have been renewed (around 3km of roadways and pathways re-surfaced and 106 new lighting columns erected),
- David Dale's Gate – a feature entrance has been created with new fencing by renowned artist Adrian Wiszniewski,
- Doulton Fountain – removed from its historic site on the Green's central avenue to a new civic space fronting the People's Palace, the fountain has been restored to its original magnificence,
- events space – new landscaping ensures that around 50% of the total area of the Green is available for festivals, performances and celebrations,
- interpretation – the Green's history, its character, culture and monuments are commemorated in

eighteen new named gateways, 'words in stone' and in new literature and IT resources,

- guided tours – the Glasgow Green Park Rangers now conduct daily tours drawing on the new interpretation resources,
- planting – 115 existing trees have been transplanted and 547 new semi-mature trees and 86 topiary yews planted,
- restoration of monuments – in addition to the McLennan Arch, the Doulton Fountain and Nelson's Monument, a further three fountains and four monumental/sculptural works have been refurbished,
- security – new fencing and lighting is augmented by CCTV and help-points to provide a safer environment for visitors, and
- Winter Gardens enclosure – provision has been made for outdoor catering; statuary from elsewhere on the Green has been restored and brought here to an enclosed garden setting amid new planting.

Bibliography

Colm Brogan, *Glasgow Story* (London, 1952)

Alasdair Buchan, *The Right to Work – The Story of the Upper Clyde Confrontation* (London, 1972)

John Burrowes, *Great Glasgow Stories* (Edinburgh, 1998)

Corporation of the City of Glasgow, *Municipal Glasgow* (Glasgow, 1914)

James Cowan, *Glasgow's Treasure Chest* (Glasgow, 1951)

David Daiches, *Glasgow* (London, 1977)

T.M. Devine, *The Tobacco Lords* (Edinburgh, 1990)

A.M. Doak and Andrew McLaren Young, *Glasgow at a Glance* (London, 4th edition, 1983)

Mary Edward, *Who Belongs to Glasgow? 200 Years of Migration* (Glasgow, 1993)

Thomas Fairbairn, *Relics of Ancient Architecture and Other Picturesque Scenes in Glasgow* (Glasgow, 1896)

Joe Fisher, *The Glasgow Encyclopaedia* (Edinburgh, 1994)

Friends of the People's Palace, *Glasgow Green and Roundabout – a Tourist Guide* (Glasgow, 1983)

Glasgow Humane Society, *Lifeboat, Rules & Guidelines for Safe Use of the River Clyde by Rowing Clubs* (Glasgow, 2005)

Glasgow Institute of Fine Arts, *Old Glasgow* (Glasgow, 1896)

Glasgow Museums, *Glasgow in the 1840s* (Glasgow Museums, 1998)

Glasgow Museums, *The People's Palace Book of Glasgow* (Edinburgh, 1998)

Malcolm Higgs, Anne Riches and Elizabeth Williamson, *The Buildings of Scotland – Glasgow* (London, 1990)

Elspeth King, *The Hidden History of Glasgow's Women – The THENEW Factor* (Edinburgh, 1993)

Elspeth King, *The People's Palace and Glasgow Green* (Edinburgh, 1991)

Elspeth King, *The Strike of the Glasgow Weavers 1787* (Glasgow, 1987)
Bill Knox and Martin Edwards, *The Lazarus Widow* (London, 1999)
Pat Lally and Neil Baxter, *Lazarus Only Done It Once* (London, 2000)
David Leslie, Ian Samuel, Alan Stewart, Harry Teggin, *Glasgow Revealed* (Scotland, 1988)
Hugh MacDonald, *Rambles Round Glasgow in the 1850s* (Glasgow, 1910, reprinted Blanefield, 1982)
Alex Matheson, *Glasgow's Other River – Exploring the Kelvin* (Ayr, 2000)
Matt McGinn, *McGinn of the Calton* (Glasgow, 1993)
Caragh McKay, *Creative Clyde* (Glasgow, 2005)
Charles McKean, David Walker, Frank Walker, *Central Glasgow – An Illustrated Architectural Guide* (Edinburgh, 1989)
Ray McKenzie, *Sculpture in Glasgow* (Glasgow, 1999)
John N. Moore, *The Maps of Glasgow* (Glasgow, 1996)
Edwin Morgan, *Collected Poems* (Manchester, 2004)
John M'Ure, *The History of Glasgow* (Glasgow, 1736, reprinted 1830)
C.A. Oakley, *The Second City – The Story of Glasgow* (Glasgow, 4th edition, 1990)
George Parsonage, *Rescue His Business The Clyde His Life – The Story of Ben Parsonage and The Glasgow Humane Society* (Glasgow, 1990)
John Riddell, *The Clyde – The Making of a River* (Edinburgh, 2000)
Senex (Robert Reid), *Old Glasgow and Its Environs* (London, 1864)
Sydney Goodsir Smith, *A Choice of Burns's Poems and Songs* (London, 1966)
Thomas Somerville, *George Square Glasgow* (Glasgow, 1891)
Hamish Whyte and George Oliver, *Mungo's Tongues* (Glasgow, 1993)

Index

Glasgow
CITY COUNCIL

The Headley Trust

HISTORIC SCOTLAND

Supported by
The National Lottery®
through the Heritage Lottery Fund

Heritage
Lottery Fund

STRATHCLYDE
european
PARTNERSHIP

The 1805 Club